Investor Relations
for the emerging company

Founded in 1807, John Wiley & Sons is the oldest independent publishing company in the United States. With offices in North America, Europe, Australia, and Asia, Wiley is globally committed to developing and marketing print and electronic products and services for our customers' professional and personal knowledge and understanding.

The Wiley Finance series contains books written specifically for finance and investment professionals as well as sophisticated individual investors and their financial advisors. Book topics range from portfolio management to e-commerce, risk management, financial engineering, valuation and financial instrument analysis, as well as much more.

For a list of available titles, please visit our Web site at *www.WileyFinance.com*.

Investor Relations
for the emerging company

RALPH A. RIEVES
and
JOHN LEFEBVRE

John Wiley & Sons, Inc.

contents

preface

THIS BOOK IS WRITTEN for officers and directors of new public companies. Its purpose is to prepare them for a task unique to business life after the initial public offering. That task is communicating about the company's commitment to enhancing shareholder value.

This book is divided into three parts. Part One describes the organizations, institutions, mechanics, and behavior of the capital markets. Chapters 2 and 3 describe the structure of the markets and review the basics of investment theories and practices. Readers with a background in these topics may choose to skip these chapters. Chapters 4, 5, and 6 are descriptive and prescriptive. The practices and procedures suggested within these chapters are grounded in the authors' experiences and upon recent empirical research.

Part Two of this book is the most descriptive and objective. Its chapters address the whys, hows, and whens of reporting and disclosure. Its focus is on legal requirements and how best to implement compliance. It is intended as a procedural guide and has been reviewed by legal experts.

Part Three evolved from the authors' investor relations consulting practice. This part of the book details how to operate an effective investor relations program within a company's budgetary restraints.

Michael Rosenbaum, an esteemed investor relations consultant, got right to the point when he observed, "Learning to deal with investors, employees, media, regulators and others in a post-IPO environment requires commitment and consistency." For the emerging company, commitment and consistency are the keys to the successful transition to financial viability. If a new firm doesn't commit to consistent communications, it will limit its options for additional capital.

acknowledgments

THROUGHOUT OUR RESEARCH, writing, and rewriting, scores of investors, clients, academics, and professionals encouraged us to see this book through to completion. The suggestions of these pre-publication readers are the value-added ingredients. Three especially deserve mention for their forbearance over the long gestation. Laurie Roop helped with the research and the rewrites, as well as handling clients while we puzzled over the stipulations of Reg. FD, the consequences of narrowed spreads, and how to fight the chat room pox. In addition to solace, Rebecca Lefebvre and Carol Rieves provided other necessary support. Rebecca was a focused and fierce proofreader and cheerleader. Carol kept the business running and priorities straight.

We are comfortable with the perspectives and prejudices we bring to this book, because they were influenced by the writings (and some admonishments) of very thoughtful and intelligent people: Peter L. Bernstein, Carolyn Brancato, James Champy, Jon Christopherson, Daniel P. Coker, Benjamin Mark Cole, Robert G. Eccles, Kenneth L. Fisher, Steven Glass, Douglas K. Harmon, Mark Levy, Howard Kalt, Andrew Kessler, Baruch Lev, Jeffrey Modesitt, Junius Peake, Theodore H. Pincus, Alfred Rappaport, Marc Robins, Lawrence W. Tuller, Michael Rosenbaum, Wayne Wagner, Robert H. Waterman, Russ Wermers, and Susan E. Woodward.

Nancy Sells of eWatch and Jennifer Russo of Luce Online helped make Part III an up-to-date and valuable guide to the practice of investor relations.

We accepted all of the candid suggestions sent from the frontlines of microcap investing; therefore, we present to the reader this "horse's mouth" guide. Thank you Nancy Barber, Tom Barry, Patrick Bradford, Doug Harman, and Ken Lucas.

The Investor Universe

CHAPTER 1

Introduction

GOING PUBLIC IS A DEFINING MOMENT. Things are radically different thereafter, because the thrust of the firm's activities becomes focused on increasing its net worth. Not just on meeting the payroll or paying the bills. Not on what can be passed on to the next generation and certainly not on being one's own boss. Now your company confronts the growth challenge.

A major aspect of this growth challenge is a compounded degree of competition. A privately owned company's strategy is, in most respects, dictated by its competition. A publicly held company's strategy is dictated by competitors *as well as by all firms competing for capital*. Those other firms are everywhere in the world.

Your company has always competed for customers. Now your company must also compete for capital. When competing for customers your company contended within a range of other companies, seldom more than a dozen. When competing for capital, you are up against 16,000 other public companies. There are few ways of differentiating your company from these others.

The price of your company's stock determines your ability to raise capital. It is indisputable that the new global capital markets will allocate scarce capital among only those companies perceived as being focused on increasing shareholder value. It follows that those companies who effectively communicate that focus will enjoy a competitive advantage in sustaining their growth.

More importantly, your new publicly owned company now confronts another set of regulators, more business reporters, and more scrutiny from the public at large. Your business is conducted in an environment more complex than the one in which you did business as a private company. The complexity of this new environment is compounded by constant advances in communications technology.

This book is intended as one of your guides to operating in your new environment. The authors, and those who assisted them, have worked to keep this book concise. We have focused on prescription. Descriptions, explanations, and anecdotes are included so that you can put our suggested policies and practices into a business perspective.

Prior to, and during, the initial public offering (IPO) process, no time was available for addressing what would follow. It was difficult enough to sustain just the daily routines of business while undergoing all the preparation necessary to bring your company public. Your investment bankers may have offered some counsel and advice, but their main responsibility was to take the company public. Accountants and lawyers were appropriately focused on the minutiae of compliance. What a difference on the morning after the IPO. Now the focus is on the parties who bought shares and those who *might* buy shares.

What "distinguishes" this book from others on investor relations is our targeted audience: the managers and directors of emerging growth companies like yours. We tried to keep in mind the problems, opportunities, and unexpected events unique to a new public company. Every suggestion has roots in real-life experience or in the empirical research of highly qualified academics.

The next two chapters are descriptive and are included for background knowledge. If you are familiar with all the players in the global capital markets, you may choose to skip these chapters.

As you read this book, keep in mind that investor relations activities are vital to growing your company. They require daily monitoring and management. Otherwise, you could find your company in legal and/or financial trouble. The authors of this book have tried to provide you with the operations manual with which to avoid that trouble.

CHAPTER 2

The Securities Markets

Note to the Reader: Readers with a basic understanding of global securities markets may choose to skip this chapter.

THE STRUCTURES OF THE MARKETS in which securities trade have changed and are changing, for the better. These changes are facilitating the movement of capital and speeding the movement of information, thus enhancing the measurement of risk. The numeric term "24/7" was introduced just in this century and is understood throughout the world as the new paradigm for the capital markets: 24 hours of trading, 7 days a week. The changes have created wider opportunity for price transparency and better execution of transactions. Better execution enhances that feature of capital markets about which you must be most mindful: *liquidity.*

Liquidity is the condition enabling investors to buy or sell shares of any stock at any time at prices that are considered fair and competitive. To be viable, capital markets must perform orderly and efficiently to ensure fair and competitive prices at all times. *The liquid feature of any specific stock is the amount of shares of that stock readily available for sale or purchase.*

Regardless of how dramatically the capital markets are changing, they will never accommodate an issue that cannot be readily traded.

Despite the impact of technology and changes to the capital markets, transactions are still conducted one of two ways: by auction or through negotiation. Both types of transaction are now conducted with more precision and dispatch, but the basic modes of interaction for each remain as they have been for centuries. Each requires some kind of market center for execution. Auction transactions and negotiated transactions are distinguished from each other by the operations of their respective *market centers.*

Established companies generally have their seasoned stocks traded by auction, the market center for which is a stock exchange. The best-known stock exchanges are the New York Stock Exchange (NYSE) and the American Stock Exchange (AMEX). Stocks of most emerging companies are traded within negotiated markets; therefore, the greater part of this chapter is devoted to discussing negotiated markets.

THE NEGOTIATED MARKETS AND THE NASD

Negotiated markets are conducted within telecommunications market centers. These centers were once referred to as the "wire markets" or the "over-the-counter bulletin board (OTCBB) markets," the latter term being the most common as well as the most inaccurate.

Negotiated markets are market-making systems without the central matching agent that is common to an auction market. The advances in telecommunications technology have affected capital markets as radically as they have in any other area of business. The cyberspace global markets are experiencing changes so rapid that these changes challenge the participants' initiatives to adapt.

The National Association of Securities Dealers, Inc. (NASD), regulates the negotiated markets. It was created in 1938 by an amendment to the Securities Exchange Act of 1934. It is a nationwide membership association of securities dealers and brokers. It is not a government agency but operates within the oversight of the Securities and Exchange Commission (SEC). The original purpose of the NASD was to function as a self-regulatory organization to establish and enforce standards and codes of practice in the trading and brokering of securities.

The NASD now regulates three categories of negotiated market activity: the Over-the-Counter Bulletin Board (OTCBB), the National Association of Securities Dealers Automated Quotations (Nasdaq) Board, and Electronic Communications Networks (ECN).

The OTCBB

The OTCBB is a quotation service displaying volume information and last-sale prices of stocks not listed or traded on Nasdaq or on a national securities exchange. The OTCBB is regulated by the NASD. The only requirement for your stock to be included on the OTCBB is that your company must file periodic reports required by the SEC (10-Ks and 10-Qs), the IRS, and other federal regulatory agencies. There need be no business relationship between your company and the participants in the OTCBB. If a broker/dealer chooses to be a market maker (one who chooses to quote prices) in your company's stock, the market maker must file NASDAQ document 15c-2-11. The market maker completes this form in consultation with you and files it with the NASD. By filing form 15c-2-11, the broker/dealer agrees to keep and maintain appropriate files (due diligence files) about your company for as long as it agrees to be a market maker for your company.

The NASD has no regulatory authority over your company. If your company fails to file a required report to a regulatory agency, it is the SEC's responsibility to deal with your filing delinquency. If a company is delinquent, the NASD just appends an "E" as a fifth letter to your listing symbol. Once the NASD has been informed that your company is again meeting all eligibility requirements, your listing symbol will revert back to four letters. If, after 60 days, the NASD has not been notified that your company is now in compliance, your stock is removed from the OTCBB.

The primary advantage for your company to be in the OTCBB system is to make it feasible for investors to purchase your stock. Another advantage is the inference that your company complies with all reporting requirements. One of the major limitations is the reluctance of institutional investors to hold OTCBB securities. The obvious disadvantage is that the OTCBB provides the least degree of market center discipline on the price of your stock.

> **OTCBB price quotes are posted electronically, but prices are not negotiated electronically. Negotiations are conducted between two parties by telephone.**

When trading is heavy, the time to complete transactions can be lengthy. Prices can be moving up or down significantly. A buy or sell market order may be booked at a price that is way off from what a customer is expecting.

Two of the NASD rules, enforced on the OTCBB to protect investors, indirectly benefit companies whose stocks are traded. These two rules provide some assurance that your stock's price is a fair representation of its supply and the demand for it:

> **THE FIRM QUOTE RULE.** A dealer can't post an "intent" to buy or sell your stock at a stated price, unless it fully intends to honor that price under conditions specified at the time of its bid or offer.

> **THE BEST EXECUTION RULE.** The broker/dealer has to prove that it exercised "reasonable diligence" in getting the best possible price for a customer. It must show that it obtained quotes from at least three dealers, or from both dealers if there are fewer than three.

Nasdaq

Even with these strictly enforced rules, there are enough limitations inherent in the OTCBB process to aspire for a more inclusive listing on Nasdaq, which began its operations in February of 1971.

The Nasdaq system collects, validates, and distributes quotation information to a subscriber base of brokers, dealers, and institutional investors. Nasdaq provides subscribers with real-time price information via electronic display for its listed stocks: the best bid and ask price, the last sales price, and volume. The newly implemented SuperSoes system permits NASD member firms to execute trades of small company stocks automatically without waiting for an exchange of messages. Nasdaq's Trade Acceptance and Reconciliation Services (TARS) simplify a listed company's procedures for transferring and clearing the transactions involving the company's stock.

Stocks accepted for listing on Nasdaq are divided into two tiers based on total market capitalization: Nasdaq National Market Issues and Nasdaq Small-Cap Issues. Emerging companies who aspire to become listed as a Nasdaq Small-Cap Issue must initially meet the following criteria:

- Retain a minimum bid price of $4 a share.
- Own $4 million in net tangible assets.
- Have a public float of at least 1 million shares.
- Have a total market valuation on the float of at least $5 million.
- Have at least 300 shareholders, each of whom must have purchased at least 100 shares or more in the open market.
- Have at least two market makers.

Once listed, any Nasdaq Small-Cap stock whose minimum bid remains below $1 per share for 30 consecutive days will be issued a 90-day warning from Nasdaq that the company is in danger of being delisted. Immediately upon receiving a warning, the company must let Nasdaq listing officials know what action and/or circumstances will raise the share price back to above $1 within 90 days. If the company cannot rectify the situation within that 90-day period, Nasdaq can move to delist. The same danger of delisting applies to falling below the minimum standards for any of the other listing requirements.

A listing on Nasdaq is evidence that your company is financially viable and that there is some measure of liquidity in the market for its stock. The stock now has some appeal for certain institutional investors.

Market Makers

A market maker is any broker/dealer firm that has posted its willingness to buy or sell a round lot (100 shares or more) of a security at the prevailing price. To retain a Nasdaq Small-Cap listing, your company needs to have at least two dealers who are willing to make a market in your stock. There are two categories of market makers: retailers and wholesalers. The Nasdaq listing staff has no rule about whether the market makers "sponsoring" your company's stock should be *retailers* or *wholesalers*.

Retail market makers are preferred but are the most difficult to attract. The retail market maker has a brokerage sales staff that will be promoting your company's stock to prospective investors who may keep the stock for a reasonable period of time. Your company's stock, therefore, must be more appealing than the other thousands of issues in terms of liquidity (that word again) as well as future prospects. If your company's stock exhibits a sustained increase in its market price, your company will have the obvious allegiance of the market maker.

An Unhappy Situation

Most emerging companies' market makers are wholesale market makers. Wholesalers make markets in thousands of stocks for other dealers and brokers. Many times wholesalers can wind up just trading stock with other traders, and the stock of your company may never get into retail distribution. This unhappy state of affairs in some way is the consequence of regulatory action taken to curb some trading abuses on Nasdaq.

In the mid-1990s, the SEC took note of allegations about collusion among traders on price quotes and additional research proving that trading costs on Nasdaq were measurably higher than trading costs on the NYSE. In 1997, Nasdaq, under the persuasion of the SEC, instituted new rules to correct the situations.

The rules caused a decrease in the spread between the *bid* (where dealers bought a stock) and the *ask* (where they sold a stock). The result was a severe diminishing of profit opportunities in trading. Many dealers stopped making markets and sent their orders to wholesalers who built their businesses on making markets in thousands of stocks.

Wholesale firms now are structured with less intent of profiting from spreads. Rather, they make money by information gleaned from analyzing the orders for a stock passing through any particular dealer's system. They try to take advantage of what the collective transactions involving that stock might reveal. These firms pay the less intrepid broker/dealers to direct the executions to them. This activity is known as "paying for order flow." Not surprisingly, there are some prominent critics of this practice.

What does this mean for your company's stock? Aside from the fact that it is difficult to find market makers who actually provide sponsorship, it means that the problems associated with your company's relatively small float are aggravated. It means that you need to know as much as you can about the future of the negotiated markets in general and the future role of market makers in particular.

THE AUCTION MARKET: STOCK EXCHANGES

Earlier in this chapter, we explained that the stocks of most emerging companies were traded within the negotiated markets and that the auction markets traded the higher-capitalized seasoned stocks. Nevertheless, the AMEX is actively recruiting emerging companies to list their stocks with it. That may signal that there are some changes occurring in long-established practices of trading stocks. There now exists the likelihood that the stock of your company could be traded on an exchange, that is, in the auction market. The auction market exchanges might become significant players in providing liquidity for stocks of companies such as yours.

The auction market, or more accurately the open-outcry auction market, is composed of the stock exchanges. The largest exchanges are the NYSE and the AMEX. A stock exchange generally conducts centralized trading in public view.

The Specialist

The members of an exchange charged with making "an orderly market" for the stocks listed on that exchange are called the specialists. The specialists have specific stocks for which they make a market. They are responsible for opening the market and for the prompt execution of orders left with them. They buy shares for and sell shares from their own account to give market depth and to provide price continuity.

The popular name for the record-keeping device used by specialists to record buy and sell orders is called "the specialist's book." In some cases, the book might be a loose-leaf notebook; or it could comprise time-stamped order tickets arranged by price. On the large exchanges, the books are computerized. Whatever the format, the book must record all customer buy and sell orders, the number of shares for each order, and the conditions or prices at which the orders are to be executed.

The perceived advantage for a stock trading in an auction market is that the trading activity of that stock is conducted by open outcry. The trading price is easily discerned throughout a trading day.

LIQUIDITY, LIQUIDITY, LIQUIDITY

Again, float size is a major concern. Whether a stock is traded within a negotiated market or on an exchange floor, the number of shares available for trading must be in a quantity large enough to permit those shares to be converted into cash without a significant loss of value.

In the next chapter, we describe and explain the behavior of the investors whose activities determine the price levels at which the stock of your company trades.

CHAPTER 3

Modern Investing Theories and Practices

Note to the Reader: This chapter is included as background for the descriptions and prescriptions detailed in the next chapter. Readers with a basic understanding of portfolio management principles and investment styles may choose to skip this chapter.

MONEY MANAGER AND FINANCIAL HISTORIAN Peter L. Bernstein has stated with his customary elegance:

Investing is a process of making decisions today whose results will not be known until tomorrow. Nobody knows what tomorrow will bring, because nobody can control everything that is going to happen tomorrow. The overarching reality, the launching pad from which investment theory takes off, is that being wrong on occasion is inescapable, even for people who are very smart. The subject matter of investment theory, then, is about why being wrong is inescapable and then about how best to manage our affairs in the face of that disagreeable reality.[1]

Bernstein could have pointed out that there is significant disagreement about how "best to manage" large pools of money among "people who are very smart." There is also agreement. We will look at the areas of agreement first.

RISK AND RETURN

Experienced professionals and academics generally agree that rational investors are primarily concerned with risk and return. An accepted definition of *risk* is the possibility that an asset will be sold at a price that is lower than the purchase price. Scholars and pros agree that diversification among selected stocks in a portfolio affect the trade-off between risk and return.

Consider two hypothetical stocks: Stock A's market price goes up when it snows and is lower when it is not snowing. Stock B's price goes up when the weather is warm and is lower when it is snowing. The return from a portfolio that holds just these two stocks, bought at the same price, will depend on the weighted holdings between the two, but there will always be some payoff. The risk of holding one stock is reduced by the reward of holding the shares of the other. Diversification has reduced the overall risk of the portfolio. It follows then that the overall risk of a particular stock isn't as much of a concern as how it affects the overall risk of the portfolio.

Picking the right stocks for the portfolio from the entire universe of stocks is the challenge, especially when you must account for investors' different levels of risk tolerance, that is, their desire for gain relative to their aversion to loss. Professor Harry Markowitz was awarded the 1990 Nobel Prize for economics for developing a statistical approach to dealing with that challenge. Professor William F. Sharpe shared the 1990 Nobel Prize because he took Markowitz's work further.

Sharpe's Capital Asset Pricing Model

Markowitz developed the means to study how investors choose among risky assets. Sharpe's contribution was the division of portfolio risk into two parts: *systematic* and *unsystematic*. Systematic risk is market-related risk. It is the risk of being in the market (the system). Systematic risk can't be diversified away. Unsystematic risk is the risk *specific* to a single stock: an unexpected decrease in earnings, a product recall, a strike, etc. This unsystematic (specific) risk can be reduced by including that asset in a portfolio of many different *(diverse)* assets.

The systematic risk of a stock is the variation of its price due to changes in the overall market. Again, Sharpe's theory holds that this market risk can't be diversified away. The specific risks of different stocks in a portfolio can be reduced by diversification strategies. These observations are part of the basis for what is now known as the *capital asset pricing model* (CAPM). How these risks relate to your investor-relations activities is discussed at length in Chapter 5. There are some controversies surrounding the CAPM; however, they deal with refinements and anomalies that academics get paid to study and that portfolio managers attempt to arbitrage.

Is the Market Efficient?

An argument exists in the world of finance in which there is a distinct dichotomy. It won't go away, and it may have some effect on the market value of your company's stock. Some people who are very smart argue that "You can't beat the market." Some other people who are very smart respond, "Yes you can."

This ongoing argument is about a theory known as the *efficient market hypothesis* (EMH). The EMH consists of four propositions. They are

1. Successive stock prices are mostly unrelated and tend to move within the market in a random manner.

2. There are many participants in the market, and they have access to all relevant information affecting stock prices.

3. Market prices fully reflect and discount all information available to the public and to investment professionals.

4. New information is quickly disseminated throughout the market.

What Market?

What does *market* mean in the context of the EMH? In the general framework of the theory, it means all exchanges and systems whose listing requirements include disclosure of relevant information about a listed company's stock. In practice, market means the arena in which company stocks of like market capitalizations are traded.

Benchmarks

EMH holds that all information about all stocks, in a defined market, is reflected in the current market prices of those stocks. It follows in the EMH argument then that no investors can consistently beat the market. This argument requires a market benchmark, or proxy, against which a given investor's performance can be measured. Each benchmark is an aggregation of carefully selected stocks that mirror a specific universe of stocks. There are several of these benchmarks computed every day as indexes or averages. The best-known benchmarks are those against which large-market-cap investors are measured, like the Dow Jones Averages and the Standard and Poor's (S&P) 500. Small-cap stock investors are usually measured against the Russell 2000.

How the performance of investors in emerging company stocks is measured is still being determined. Never mind. That is not why we are discussing EMH with you. The relevance of this discussion, for you, is that there are some professional investors who will *never be targets* for your investor-relations activities.

Passive Investing

Proponents of the EMH argue that because all investors are part of the market, their collective actions will cancel each other out. The EMH adherents think that any investment return will, over time, revert to the mean, best represented by a benchmark. The extension of that mind-set is that a portfolio should hold only those stocks in the benchmark aggregate. This portfolio strategy is called *indexing* or *passive investing*. Thirty percent of institutional stock portfolios are passively managed. This means that

> **About one-third of all institutional investment managers will never be interested in your company's stock, regardless of its market cap.**

Active Investing

There are a lot of portfolio managers who think their respective investment strategies can outperform a given benchmark and that they can sustain their performance. They think they can beat the market. They argue that when one-third of portfolio managers invest in index funds, that leaves opportunities for those who really know how to research companies and stocks. If someone's efforts can determine whether a stock's price is really an indication of its value, then that someone can make investors a lot of money. That someone is adding value to the investment process. "C'est moi!"

INVESTMENT STYLES

How an active investment manager tries to add value to portfolios of stock is the major concern of present and prospective clients. This concern is not just about returns besting the indexers but also about diversification.

Professional investors believe that the market prices of different assets (stocks, bonds, real estate, etc.) move in different directions, depending on the overall economic climate. Fiduciaries of pension funds, foundations, and endowments, therefore, want diversification among different asset classes These professionals even want diversification *within an asset class,* such as stocks. They want to diversify their "stock" money among portfolio managers that specialize in stocks of a certain type. That specialization is referred to in the financial world as *style.*

Some managers focus on particular industries and are referred to as *sector-style* managers. Others focus on stocks whose growth in earnings has exceeded the average growth rate of all stocks— hence they are called *growth-stock* managers. Portfolio managers investing in stocks they believe are presently undervalued are known as *value-style* managers. Growth and value are the most common style categories. For an obvious reason, growth investors are discussed in great detail in Chapter 4.

Value Investors

Value investors focus on a company's *book value,* which in its simplest form is calculated as total assets minus all liabilities and intangibles like goodwill and the par value of any restricted treasury stock. The other commonly accepted terms for this value are *net tangible value* and *liquidating value.*

After value portfolio managers have calculated the book values of selected stocks, they compare them to their present market prices. If the market price of a stock is significantly less than the computed book value, that particular stock is a candidate for the portfolio. The manager would further search for reasons why that stock appears to be undervalued. The rationale for the value style of investing is the assumption that, at some time, other investors will recognize that the stock is undervalued. Their subsequent purchases would raise the value of the shares that are already in the manager's portfolio.

Value managers usually restrict their research and investments within a specific market capitalization grouping. There are large-cap value managers, medium-cap value managers, and small-cap value managers.

You may correctly infer that there are no value managers for emerging companies, because they are looking for the stocks of *re-emerging* companies. The purpose of the foregoing was to explain what value managers act like. If you encounter some, you now know not to waste your time discussing the merits of your stock.

Growth Investors

Growth portfolio managers focus on sustained growth in earnings. They look for companies whose annual earnings increase at a rate greater than the market as a whole. These pros spend a lot of time and money searching for those companies whose growth rates, current and projected, are not fully reflected in the price of their stock. Their opportunities to discover a stock before other investors do are significantly fewer than those of value investors. Earnings rates are easy to identify; therefore, there are more investors in the hunt for the growth stocks. Time can be the friend of the value investor but never the friend of the growth investor.

Growth portfolio managers have a heightened sense of urgency, hence they spend a lot of time and money to get an earlier position in a stock. They restrict their investing within a specific market-capitalization grouping, categorizing themselves as large-cap growth, medium-cap growth, small-cap growth, or microcap growth. The latter is a very distinct group from which you can find investors who will talk with you about your stock.

Investing is all about risk and proportionate return. The next chapter is about professional investors who deal with the issues of risk and reward. The purpose of the next chapter is to assist you in identifying, among those thousands of professionals, the ones who will want to buy your company's stock.

NOTE

1. Peter L. Bernstein, ed. *The Portable MBA in Investment* (New York, NY: John Wiley & Sons, 1995).

Institutional Investors

CHAPTER 3 DESCRIBES SOME THEORIES AND PRACTICES that experienced investors use in developing an investment strategy. The purpose of Chapter 4 is to explain which investors have the objective of buying thousands of shares of emerging companies' securities. This selectively targeted group is a very small part of the largest and most important segment of the investing world, the *institutional investor community*.

Our definition of an *institutional investor* is a person or an organization that assumes the responsibility of investing, or overseeing the investment of large pools of money. The institutional investor community includes all the fiduciary parties and all the parties who provide services to fiduciaries. This includes investment managers, brokers, custodians, researchers, software vendors, consultants, accountants, and attorneys.

YOUR COMPANY MUST BE LISTED

If your company stock is not listed for trading on an exchange or on the Nasdaq Small-Cap Market System, it is not considered a viable investment by most institutional investors. A listed stock's value is openly negotiated, and the most recent price at which the stock trades is available immediately. A major concern of institutions is liquidity. Listed stocks must have a minimum float of 1 million public shares, thus ensuring some liquidity.

Stocks listed on an exchange or the Nasdaq system are also subject to strictly defined financial reporting and disclosure requirements. See Table 4–1. OTCBB stocks are also subject to the same

TABLE 4–1 The Nasdaq Small-Cap Market Requirements

A company must meet minimum financial requirements for initial listing and continue to meet standards to maintain their listing on the Nasdaq Small-Cap Market.

Requirements	Initial Listing	Continued Listing
Net Tangible Assets[1]	$4 million	$2 million
	or	or
Market Capitalization	$50 million	$35 million
	or	or
Net Income (in latest fiscal year or 2 of last 3 fiscal years)	$750,000	$500,000
Public Float (shares)[2]	1 million	500,000
Market Value of Public Float	$5 million	$1 million
Minimum Bid Price	$4	$1
Shareholders (round lot holders)[3]	300	300
Operating History	1 year	N/A
	or	
Market Capitalization	$50 million	
Market Makers[4]	3	2
Corporate Governance	Yes	Yes

[1] Net Tangible Assets equals Total Assets minus Total Liabilities minus Goodwill minus Redeemable Securities.
[2] Public float is defined as shares that are not held directly or indirectly by any officer or director of the issuer and by any other person who is the beneficial owner of more than 10 percent of the total shares outstanding.
[3] Round lot holders are considered holders of 100 shares or more.
[4] An Electronic Communications Network (ECN) is not considered an active Market Maker.

reporting and disclosure requirements, but they don't provide three essential features necessary for institutional investor appeal: liquidity, liquidity, and liquidity.

> **Until your company meets the requirements for public listing and attains that status, do not expect any interest from the institutional investor community.**

THE INSTITUTIONAL BUY SIDE

Two-thirds of institutionally managed money is composed of retirement funds. The other common pools of money are insurance companies, corporate treasuries, endowments, foundations, and the assets of high-net-worth individuals. The latter pool has increased significantly since 1990.

The professionals who aspire to invest these pools of money for a fee include mutual funds, brokerage firms, independent money managers, bank trust departments, and insurance companies. Publicly owned mutual funds are the most common investment organizations. Mutual funds are legal entities that are usually sponsored or owned by banks, brokers, independent money managers, and insurance companies.

These fiduciaries and investment professionals are known collectively as the *buy side.* They, in turn, are the customers for professionals, like stockbrokers, who provide services. Those third parties are known collectively as the *sell side.*

Most of this chapter will be devoted to the buy side. Why this is so will become apparent if we take a few pages to first discuss the sell side.

THE INSTITUTIONAL SELL SIDE

Broker/dealer and investment banking firms make up most of the sell side segment of the institutional investment community. They sell their intermediary services and research services to the investment decision makers in return for commissions and fees.

Sell Side Research

Sell side research firms maintain extensive research departments. A research department is composed of *economists* (who study global and national economic trends), *technical analysts* (who watch security price movements and the movement of selected indexes to forecast a direction in which these values will move), and *company security analysts.* Company security analysts and their support staff account for most of the people employed in a research department. They are the heart of a sell side research department.

These analysts, who conduct research and recommend the purchase or sales of securities, specialize in a particular industry or sector. According to research from Nelson Information, there are now about 1,600 security analysts employed among the top 25 broker/dealers. There were about 900 in 1994.

From an organizational point of view, these analysts are supposed to provide the brokerage clients of their firms with informed opinions about the present and future market price of a company's stock. Sell side security analysts with reputations for "good calls" are among the highest-paid people in the investment business.

Since the 1990s, this high level of compensation has not been due to just "good calls." There is another reason for "taking care" of a high-profile analyst. This reason has roots in the recent and large changes that have occurred in the capital markets.

The Sell Side Dilemma

Recent events have had a severe impact on the full-service broker/ dealer houses in the United States and Western Europe. Full-service firms, as recently as the early 1990s, could depend on "dense" profits from five areas of revenue: brokerage commissions, dealer (trading) profits, derivatives activities, money management fees, and fees earned from investment banking.

Competition among established stock brokerage firms, the discount houses, and the on-line trading services has reduced revenue streams from the established firms' brokerage commissions. More importantly, these firms have watched the diminishment of the high-profit leverage that used to characterize commission revenues.

The advent of the decimal pricing system has further narrowed the bid-ask spreads of traded securities, thus making it more difficult for the dealer side of the firms to earn large profits on spreads. Firms are already shifting to "order flow" strategies in an attempt to create profits on momentum volume.

The staffing of "rocket science" talent throughout the derivatives strategy departments of all the major firms has diluted the competitive advantage that any one firm may have had in the trading or development of synthetic securities.

Profits earned from the money management business have decreased over the last decade to about 1 percent of the assets managed. The pressure of earning profit margins in the investment management business has evolved into an economy-of-scale challenge. Merger activities among sell side and buy side investment managers is your evidence. (These mergers of large investment managers may be of some advantage to your emerging company, as we will discuss in Chapter 5.)

The remaining activity for dense profit revenues is investment banking. This category includes underwriting and merger-acquisition operations. Not surprisingly, investment banking is very competitive. Because most of the integrated securities firms have the same capabilities and sources of capital, success is dependent on the quality of the relationships a firm's investment bankers maintain with top corporate management.

Don't Misinterpret

Don't misinterpret this business fact of life: A close relationship between banker X and company Y's CEO won't necessarily ensure that X will be Y's investment banker of choice. It can, however, assure X the opportunity to be the first to learn about Y's corporate strategy and promote X's capabilities in implementing the financial aspects of that strategy.

The Tightrope

In October 1999, SEC Chairman Arthur Levitt addressed the Economic Club of New York. During this talk, he cited a memo from an unnamed, full-service Wall Street firm that read in part: "We do not make negative or controversial comments about our [banking] clients as a matter of sound business policy." Levitt then remarked that an analyst "walks a tightrope" by writing an unbiased report about a company with whom his or her firm's bankers have a relationship.

Every year the Boston research firm Thomson Financial First Call releases a survey of 28,000 research reports. Every survey has shown that fewer than 1 percent of the reports specifically recommended selling a company's stock.

A logical inference is that an analyst might slant a research report in a way that reinforces the analyst's banking colleagues' relationship with the company. That, however, is not the main concern as an executive of an emerging company.

If there are conflicts of interest within securities firms that continue to diminish the veracity of investor information, the situation will be redressed sooner or later by the SEC, or the self-regulatory bodies like the exchanges and the NASD. The October 2000 SEC regulation about fair disclosure (Reg. FD) is an example.

A Real Fact of Public Company Life

What won't be redressed is the manner in which analysts and investment bankers work together. *Here is a real fact of public company life:*

Your emerging company will receive no research attention from a major sell side firm if you can't provide some big bucks business for that firm's investment bankers.

You may be invited to make presentations at a broker/dealer-sponsored conference. A firm's broker, working on his or her own initiative, could promote your securities to the broker's clients. If you have no prospects for a multimillion-dollar secondary offering, an acquisition strategy, or of being acquired, your chances of being featured in a sell side report by a major firm are zero.

Concentrate on the buy side!

SELECTED TARGETING WITHIN THE BUY SIDE

The overriding concern of any business, large or emerging, is the efficient use of resources and the elimination of waste. Your investor relations program should be as subject to process discipline as any other corporate function. This is a point that Theodore H. Pincus has been emphasizing since the early 1990s. Pincus is the founder and chairman emeritus of The Financial Relations Board, Inc., and is regarded as the "Dean" of investor-relations (IR) professionals. Among the qualities that have earned this esteem is Pincus's prescience.

He was the first IR professional to recommend going directly to the buy side.

The key to efficient and effective IR is *selected targeting* of institutional investors. You have made the first step by eliminating the sell side analysts. Additionally, there are some easy "exclusions" to make among the buy side players. Two obvious categories are funds that specialize in foreign stocks and the indexers (passive investors). Because your company is an emerging company, not a *re*-emerging company, also eliminate those investment managers that restrict their activities to value strategies.

Using your knowledge about institutional investors, you have just eliminated all the sell side, all the indexers, all the portfolio managers who focus on foreign stocks, and all the value players. Now, you can begin the winnowing of buy side growth investors.

Growth Investors

Growth companies are defined in Chapter 3 as companies whose annual earnings increase at a rate greater than the market as a whole. Growth investment managers look for companies whose earnings growth rates are not fully reflected in the price of their stocks. They will look even further among such companies to find those that fit one of four subcategories. Each of these subcategories is distinguished within a given range of market-capitalization values: large-cap growth stocks, medium-cap growth stocks, small-cap growth stocks, and microcap growth stocks. See Table 4–2.

Why do most managers of growth portfolios focus on only one type of market-cap stock? The short explanation for this behavior is that pension plan sponsors (and other fiduciaries) believe that the level of a stock's market capitalization will determine how that stock's value will fluctuate under varying economic and market conditions.

Remember that the goal of any owner of a large pool of assets is diversification among money managers. These fiduciaries want diversification even within investment styles. They want to hold different growth funds. Each fund should be different from the other by specializing in *just one* range of market-cap stocks. Big money will feel more protected under varying economic and market conditions especially if they have diversified their growth strategies among these specialized portfolios.

Growth-style managers learned they could more easily acquire clients if they differentiated themselves by market-cap specialization.

The market capitalization ranges that dictate the size category of a stock are shown in Table 4–2.

TABLE 4-2   Stock Categories by Market Capitalization

(Shares Outstanding × Current Market Price)

Large Cap	More than $5 billion
Medium Cap	Between $1.5 billion and $5 billion
Small Cap	Between $1.5 billion and $300 million
Microcap	Less than $300 million

The market cap of your emerging company is most likely to be in the microcap category. The next chapter is devoted to what you need to know to get the attention and support of your targeted institutional investors: *the Microcap Growth Investment Manager.*

CHAPTER 5

Targeting the Microcap Growth Investment Manager

MICROCAP STOCK IS ONE OF THE NEWEST TERMS in the language of investing. The authors first encountered the word "microcap" as it was used by John Markese (president of the American Association of Individual Investors) on *Adam Smith's Money World* in early 1996. The first conference for institutional investors on microcap stocks was held that year. This term is so new that there is still more than one accepted spelling: microcap and micro-cap. We use the spelling that has been consistently used by The Bloomberg Press, a division of the financial data and communications company Bloomberg L.P.

Table 4–2 shows that any stock with a market capitalization of less than $300 million is classified as a microcap stock. Small company stocks with very low market caps have been around for a long time. Until recently, they were never traded on exchanges but rather among a loosely affiliated group of brokers and traders generally referred to as the Over-the-Counter Market or more frequently the "OTC." Closing OTC stocks' bid and ask prices from the previous day got published every business morning by the National Quotations Bureau (NQB) on sheets of pink paper. (NQB prices are now distributed electronically.) These stocks were most often referred to as "Pink Sheet" stocks. Whether or not they deserved to be characterized as such, these stocks were considered speculative investments. The NASD arranged for those companies who agreed to file periodic financial reports required by the SEC to be designated and traded as OTCBB stocks. As discussed in Chapter 2, operating strictures precluded almost all institutional investors from investing in the smallest of market-cap stocks.

Two factors, among the many changes and events occurring in the capital markets in the 1990s, created explosive institutional interest in this unique class of common stocks. These two factors were the burgeoning of initial public offerings (IPOs) and the establishment of the Nasdaq Small-Cap Market System.

BURGEONING IPOs

A convergence of situations and events in the 1990s created one of the most favorable environments for investing in stocks in capital markets' history. This happy set of circumstances has been the subject of hundreds of articles and, recently, dozens of books. Key factors were the demand for stock funds by members of defined-contribution retirement plans (such as 401(k)s, a reduction in capital gains taxes, and low inflation. What has distinguished this bull market from previous sustained enthusiasm was the great demand for stock with small market capitalizations.

THE DEMAND FOR SMALL-CAP AND MICROCAP STOCKS

The rapid advances in information and biological technology were being created, for the most part, among small groups of academics, innovators, and inventors, few of whom were working within the confines of the established corporations that have been the dominant forces in business and industry. These new enterprises needed capital. Because there were increasing demands for new investment opportunities, the time was right for acquiring capital. Most of the capital was acquired from venture investors whose aims were to eventually take the firms public for more money than they put up. Recent history records that many of those expectations have been exceeded.

THE ADVENT OF MICROCAP FUNDS

Because seasoned stocks of established companies were being traded at record highs in the mid-1990s, individual and institutional investors had to look at the stocks of these newer and smaller companies for the prospects of higher returns. The demand for these stocks drove their prices up and attracted even more money.

Not surprisingly, the mutual funds jumped in to offer smaller-cap growth portfolios to meet the demand. They eventually set up special aggressive growth portfolios and called them microcap funds. The model for these funds were the portfolios run by a handful of investment managers who had been outperforming most of the markets by painstakingly investing in emerging companies over several years. A style that had been politely viewed by the money management establishment as unconventional (and less politely viewed as "something they do in the sticks") was now an accepted strategy. A new breed of professional investors weren't attempting to be the next Peter Lynch. They wanted to be a microcap superstar.

There were about 50 microcap funds started in 1997 alone. The microcap style is to pick stocks of companies that can grow their earnings at a much faster rate than larger companies could. Overnight there were institutional buyers of emerging company stocks.

These new funds were buying selected stocks in quantities of 5,000 shares and up. They had to have market liquidity and transparent pricing. The "Pink Sheet" method of purchasing stocks couldn't accommodate these requirements. A different marketplace was evolving.

The Nasdaq Small-Cap Market System

Chapter 2 describes the development of the Nasdaq system as established in 1973. It quickly became the predominant negotiated marketplace for stocks. The success of the system required continued refinements. There now exist two distinct groupings of Nasdaq stocks: Nasdaq National Market System (NNMS) and Nasdaq Small-Cap Market System (NSCMS). In 1982, the NSCMS was introduced to facilitate the trading of stocks of emerging companies that met certain requirements. See Table 4–1 on page 26. The American Stock Exchange (AMEX) also provides the opportunity to selected emerging companies to list their securities on an auction market exchange under similar standards. Recall that in addition to meeting these standards, companies are required to follow the filing and disclosure dictates of the SEC with respect to financial information.

These new growth-style portfolios, the microcap group, now had marketplaces in which they could operate with the assurance of open pricing and some liquidity. They were also assured that the financial information about these companies would be as readily available as the information regarding large-cap stocks.

A Nimble Group of Buyers

The recent concerns of the largest mutual funds about operating with economies of scale have resulted in a number of recent mergers. The resulting investment behemoths may be enjoying economies of scale, but their trading decisions have become more bureaucratic. Bureaucracies ponder. They aren't nimble. Few of the mergers involved microcap funds. Microcap investment managers remain a nimble group of competitors for large pools of money. They are ready buyers for emerging company stocks that meet their selection criteria.

SELLING TO THE MICROCAP GROWTH MANAGERS

In Chapter 4, we said that an IR program should be as subject to process discipline as any other business function. Selling is the business function that is most like microcap IR. The overriding discipline in selling is "know your customer." Microcap investment managers are customers. They may be working in a mutual fund company or they may be independent money managers. Knowledge of how these professionals do business is essential to your effective and sustained IR program. Keep in mind that investment managers are running a business, just like you. You share the same overriding concerns: controlling costs and increasing revenues and earnings.

The Killer Costs of Managing a Microcap Portfolio

Most of the operating costs that a microcap investment manager has are similar to those of any business: facilities, personnel, marketing, communications, and the like. These can be managed with prudent attention to purchasing, hiring, and compensation practices. The costs that override the degree of success any investor has are the costs associated with buying and selling securities. These costs are referred to in the aggregate as *transaction costs*. Growth managers investing in small companies encounter higher transactions costs than any other investment style, and microcap growth managers face the highest costs of all.

Other than brokerage commissions, what other transaction costs are there? Wayne H. Wagner and Steven Glass of the Plexus Consulting Group identified and explained them in an article in the *Journal of Investment Consulting*:[1] market impact costs, delay costs, and opportunity costs.

MARKET IMPACT COSTS.　Market impact costs are measured by taking the difference in the quoted price of a stock when the manager placed an order and when the order was executed. Because microcap stocks have relatively small floats and volume, a large buy order can drive the price of the issue way up, and a sell order can drive the price way down.

DELAY COSTS.　Again, because of thin-float volatility, microcap portfolio managers may wait for the "best price" to make a trade with a market maker who is closely monitoring the stock. The odds are about even that they will not get a better price. In the worst case, they will find themselves chasing the stock or canceling the order.

OPPORTUNITY COSTS. Opportunity costs are the extreme of delay costs. They are the cost of missing out, or just partially completing an order.

An Aggressive and Expensive Investment Style

What is the common factor that governs these costs? The size of the "float." A quick quiz follows. Name three features of a stock that appeal to a portfolio manager. The answer, again, is liquidity, liquidity, and liquidity.

A growth style of investing is an aggressive style. Growth managers are "tracking" hunters. Value managers are "sit and wait" hunters, or shoppers. Tracking is, by nature, a more expensive activity than sitting. Wagner and Glass measured the aggregate transaction costs across four styles of portfolio managers: large-cap value, small-cap value, large-cap growth, and small-cap growth. The costs for a small-cap growth manager were more than four times those of a large-cap value manager and two times more than a large-cap growth or small-cap value manager.

Bad News and Good News

Some investment managers can be compared to pilots of commercial jumbo jets. Not microcap managers. They are like test pilots, the same as the founders and principals of emerging companies. They are your kin. They are big-time risk takers.

For an emerging company, here is some bad news and some good news. The bad news is that it is very expensive for an institutional investor to buy your stock. The good news is that it is very expensive for an institutional investor to sell your stock. When you finish reading this chapter, you might conclude that the good news is even better than you thought.

The Profit Challenge for Microcap Growth Managers

The burden of high costs borne by customers of your stock *is offset only by superior investment returns,* which in turn attracts more money into the microcap growth funds. Always remember that microcap growth portfolios have to significantly outperform other portfolios just to remain even within comparative cost ratios. You must understand how microcap growth investment managers operate as they attempt to outperform all other managers in the institutional universe.

Microcap Growth Managers Don't Delegate Their Research

The buck starts and stops at the microcap portfolio managers' desks. There is almost no sell side research available to them. Analysts capable of selecting outperforming stocks are very expensive to hire, train, or retain. There are only two staffing models in microcap managers' offices: Very lean or none.

You have to make it easy for the managers interested in your company to get the answers they want. These investment pros don't have time to stay on "hold." You need to organize your investor-relations team, and phone system, in a manner that permits the investment managers to reach you directly. If you can't take a call, make sure that you or a senior executive gets back to the caller within an hour.

Investment Disciplines Can Vary among Microcap Growth Managers

All managers are seeking superior returns, but they will have different selection criteria and search patterns. All want a high rate of annual earnings growth (20 percent plus) but will look at that in the context of another operating measure. Some favor high rates of revenue growth (20 percent plus), some will look for annual increases in free cash flow, and others want a pattern of increasing operating margins. Don't approach a manager until you understand that manager's selection criteria. Read the manager's prospectus and sales literature. Search the Web for transcripts of interviews the media has conducted with the target manager.

Several managers only use computer-based screening models to select stocks. They rely on statistical data about some feature they use to select stocks. Their selections are made by searching through the data for that feature among thousands of stocks. In its marketing, this kind of fund is very specific about its "proprietary screening" model. Don't waste time contacting these managers. Your company's stock will either pop up within the model or it won't.

Now What?

Closing the sale—that is, attaining the goal of institutional ownership—is an important step in enhancing the viability of an emerging company. That achievement isn't an investor-relations accomplishment in the literal sense.

Prior to the purchase of your company's stock, the investment manager wasn't an investor. Previously, you were a suitor. Now you and the manager are married. How can you manage this relationship so that you can stay married?

Truly Understanding the Microcap Growth Manager

The relationship with your institutional stockholders and their competition depends not just on the continued success and growth of the company but also on your company's policies, practices, and behavior. All this should be based on a deep understanding of the risks microcap growth portfolio managers encounter.

All investment managers work in an environment influenced by three types of risk. Two of these risks are discussed in Chapter 3: systematic (market) risk and the specific risk (unsystematic) associated with the market valuation of any stock the managers own.

Investment managers are susceptible to what can be termed *consensus risk*. Consensus risk is a branch of specific risk. It is the risk by which a stock's market value is determined, not by fundamental measures, but by the collective, and perhaps capricious, opinions of some analysts and investing peers. The remainder of this chapter discusses these three types of risk with respect to your company's stock. These risks are the elements that constitute Peter Bernstein's "disagreeable reality" in Chapter 3.

ECONOMIC NEWS AND SYSTEMATIC (MARKET) RISK

The "top guns" who run microcap portfolios believe that they (contrary to some academic theories) can outperform the overall market, even against the headwinds of high transaction costs.

Moreover, bad economic news always drives down the market values of small company stocks first. Your payroll is a bigger portion of your company's overall costs than it is in a large corporation, so news of rising wages is not good news about your company. Any news of an increase in inflation is worse news for you because the perception is that your firm has less "wiggle room" in the face of higher costs. Microcap portfolio managers are contrarians. They make money buying on the dips. Look for buying patterns in a down cycle. If you discern some buying activity in stocks like yours, crank up the IR activity.

THE RISKS SPECIFIC TO OWNING
YOUR COMPANY'S STOCK

Vigorous debates about the valuations of Web-based businesses, at one time, dominated investment news. When reviewing the comments by market professionals and academics about this matter, you come to one of two conclusions: that each party had a responsible point of view or that nobody had a clue. This section's focus is on those operating, financial, and accounting measures that are the *practical day-to-day concerns about the specific risks* of owning any emerging company's stocks.

The most frequently mentioned valuation measure in the popular media is a share price to earnings ratio, the P/E ratio. Your target investors never will accept the size of a P/E ratio as even a "first-cut" measure. Is your company, with a trailing P/E ratio of 20, a better value than Company X with 30? Probably not, if your earnings have been growing at an annual rate of 25 percent and X's have been growing at an annual rate of 50 percent.

Earlier in this chapter we said that all managers want a high rate of earnings growth but will look closely at other operating measures. Three of these other operating measures (that are of concern to microcap growth managers) are the rate of revenue growth, increase in operating margins, and an increase in free cash flow.

Growth in Revenues

Some investment managers believe so strongly that growth in revenues is the guiding measure when valuing a company that they pay a lot of attention to the *price to sales ratio*. This ratio is computed in the same manner as the P/E ratio, substituting revenues per share as the denominator. These managers cite a major reason for focusing on increasing revenues. They prefer that your company reinvest a major portion of operating margins into furthering growth. They also reason that a well-managed company continues to operate more cost efficiently; therefore, increasing revenues ensures proportionately greater margins.

These higher-leveraged revenues can be critical to how these managers value your company. Writer Magnus Buchan touched on this in an excellent article in *Red Herring* magazine:[2] "[T]he costs of processing and transmitting data (the bread-and-butter operations of many net firms) are plunging all the time, which means that sustaining rapid revenue growth becomes the key to profitability and high stock prices . . . ."

Later in the article, Buchan addressed the risk aspect: "When a company's revenue growth slows . . . investors are then more likely to value the company in line with its earnings and bail out if it looks like profits will never materialize." A couple of quarters of increased earnings, with flat revenues, can be acceptable to some portfolio managers but are a major source of concern for those who focus on the top line. They want increasing annual rates of growth in customers, unit volume, and billings. These shareholders stay awake worrying about companies that have just a few customers accounting for a large percentage of sales.

Operating Margins

Some portfolio managers look closer at the other side of the revenue/expense relationship. At some point, they want clear evidence of a return on expenses. They begin looking for productivity gains relative to your personnel costs and for higher sales from your increased advertising expenditures. They will be paying particular attention to how your research and development costs are amortized. These managers can be characterized as test pilots from Scotland. If you have a year or two when expenses have increased at a higher rate than revenues, they perceive that condition as unacceptable risk. One of these microcap growth portfolio managers told the authors, "I'm very partial to inverted burn rates." The shareholders with these portfolios require the most stroking.

Free Cash Flow

Managers of microcap growth portfolios can hardly be characterized as risk adverse; however, some of them are more cautious than their peers. These managers only look at companies that have been in business long enough to have generated *free cash flow*.

This measure is computed by first identifying your earnings before any noncash deductions, such as depreciation. From these cash earnings, the investment manager subtracts your capital investments such as equipment, buildings, and debt payments. They are, in effect, treating all your capitalization entries as expenses. Some investors, however, won't deduct certain amortizations. How they conduct their computations is not as important as understanding their "risk mind-set." They focus on cash. Where it is. Where it comes from. Where it is going. What does that mind-set mean to you? It means that if the average age of your receivables increases or your inventory begins inflating, they will sell your stock.

Balance Sheet

The risk measures described in the foregoing are items reported in just two of three financial documents: The Profit and Loss Statement and the Statement of Cash Flows. The foregoing descriptions were of operating measures. There is no intention by the authors to imply that microcap growth portfolio managers don't look at your balance sheet. They do, and the debt-to-equity ratio is one of the first items upon which they focus. They get concerned about companies that have more than 50 percent of their capital in the form of debt. Interest expense is a very specific risk.

Another item of primary interest is working capital. This is also called the current ratio and is computed by dividing current assets by current liabilities. It closely relates to cash flow. High-strung portfolio pilots need *at least* one-and-a-half times as many current assets as current liabilities to remain calm. Twice as many assets are very soothing.

The most important balance sheet item is often the most overlooked. Do your sequential balance sheets show increases in shareholder equity?

Qualitative Considerations

Of course, experienced money managers won't rely solely on operating and accounting measures. Here are some prejudices and preferences you should remember. Your targeted investors will always favor companies in which management has a large ownership stake. One portfolio manager who worked with us on this book was unambiguous: "If they are not owners, we aren't buyers."

They obviously don't like products or services that might become obsolete. They prefer that you are operating in a business with high barriers to entry. They will assume and verify that you are complying with all applicable laws and regulations. Employee turnover rates are always of interest. They also have very long memories of people who burned them with inaccurate information or who improperly managed other enterprises. Microcap growth investors are nice people but not very forgiving.

M & A Considerations

Mergers and acquisitions are always in the forefront of any experienced investor's mind. There is an estimate floating around Wall Street that for every company that goes public, there are six that get merged. Confront another fact of public-company life. You have individual and institutional shareholders that bought your stock because they think you are an attractive acquisition target.

What if your own strategy consists of plans to grow by acquisition? In the authors' experience, the pros are skeptical about that path to growth. One of the reasons for their attitude is that they want to know who conceived the strategy, you or an investment banker?

What will be the real benefits of this action?

1. Economies of scale?
2. Increased market share?
3. Synergy-driven increases in revenues, earnings, and free cash flow?
4. Will you overpay?
5. Will you lose focus on the activities that really drive your company's growth?
6. Do you have the depth of executive talent to manage a larger company?

If you intend to disclose acquisition plans to your shareholders, be prepared to answer these questions in great detail. When acquisitions are publicly announced, the market price of the acquirer usually drops. You want your institutions to stay on board. An important factor in retaining them is to ensure that you and the directors have been very deliberate in developing this strategy.

If you are in an industry fragmented among many small companies, you may have plans to acquire your competitors. This is commonly called a *rollup* strategy. Portfolio managers are even more skeptical about this approach to growth.

The Rest of This Chapter

The discussion of market risk and the specific risks of owning your company has been based on concepts and practices that are easily understood by businesspeople. We may not have told you anything you didn't already know. The challenge in writing about those risks was in making them relevant to your concerns.

The challenge in writing the rest of this chapter was in trying to explain some behavior and activities that are perplexing.

CONSENSUS RISK

Consensus risk is the risk that the market value of your company's stock is determined by the collective, and sometimes capricious, opinion of a majority of analysts and portfolio managers. Remember Peter Bernstein's observation about investment management: "[B]eing wrong on occasion is inescapable." Our discussion of *consensus* risk can best be followed if you keep in mind another observation from our own experience:

> **When, on occasion, you are wrong about a certain matter and so is everybody else, you won't get much blame.**

The Signaling Model of Investor Behavior

Risk, by definition, can be priced. Uncertainty, by definition, can't. When investors are uncertain about the prospects of a stock, they are likely to use other investors' actions as credible signals about that stock's risk-value profile. This type of behavior is referred to by academics as the *signaling model* of investor behavior.

A prime objective of this book is to tell you how to reduce the uncertainty about the prospects for your company's stocks. Avoiding being the subject of the signaling model is a function of your disclosure policies, practices, and behavior. Chapter 8 describes and recommends the best policies and practices to follow in complying with disclosure regulations, including SEC Regulation *FD (fair disclosure)*. What follows in this chapter is recommended behavior in the context of consensus risk.

Herding

When there is scant precise information about the future of a company, professional investors are subject to the signaling model. An observable effect of signaling behavior is the tendency of investment managers to move in tandem, or to *herd*. That herding exists was confirmed in a study of mutual funds by Professor Russ Wermers of the University of Maryland. The results of this study were published in the April 1999 issue of the *Journal of Finance*.[3] Professor Wermers broke his study down into subgroups of funds and subgroups of stocks. Among what group do you suspect he found the highest level of herding? Which stocks were the most likely to be subject to herding transactions? Your suspicions are confirmed. Growth-oriented funds have the highest incidence of herding, and small-cap stocks were most likely to be traded among the herds.

Wermers's study covered a 20-year period between 1975 and 1994, so there were no microcap managers or stocks represented in the study. The authors have talked with Professor Wermers on several occasions about his research. He agrees that the small floats that characterize stocks like those of your company might preclude their being subject to herding activity. It's very expensive for the portfolio manager to sell your stock. This news appears even better, but only over a very short term. As your company grows, its float and market capitalization continue to increase. At some point during that growth, the stock is likely to be subject to signaling behavior and herding transactions. Get ready.

What's the Big Deal?

Regular readers and viewers of investment news know the horror stories about money managers all dumping a stock, because the company reported quarterly earnings that disappointed sell side analysts. Since it's been established that your company is not covered by sell side analysts, so what? Again, if your company has a future, you could be confronted with this dilemma. Foreknowledge of its elements can enhance your ability to deal with another fact of public-company life. Remember Peter Bernstein's lament about what investors face? Get ready for your own "very disagreeable reality."

The Cockroach Signal

"If you see one cockroach, that means there are a lot more." This coarse observation has achieved axiom status among institutional investors. They believe that one disappointing quarterly report indicates that the company is in trouble.

One Wall Street small-stock strategist confirmed this consensus bias:

> *More often than not, an earnings shock in small stocks is the beginning of a long period of underperformance and may be the beginning of the end. It's wiser not to wait around for things to improve.*

That no one points to any empirical study for confirmation is immaterial. Wall Street has bought the cockroach signal. The SEC's Regulation FD doesn't preclude herding behavior or believing in the cockroach signal. What if all the pros did run for the exit and then the dumped company's performance greatly improves over subsequent quarters? If they were all wrong, who's to blame?

We know it takes guts to be a growth stock portfolio manager. Here is one other coarse observation. To be a contrarian growth stock portfolio manager takes more guts than a slaughterhouse has.

The Forecasting Game

"Vicious Circle" is a trite but appropriate term for the cockroach dilemma. Realizing that the pros can overreact to earnings "surprises," companies attempt to manage their earnings on a quarterly basis. Manipulation can follow and so can the scandal of accounting fraud. Financial reporting scandals receive major news coverage partly because they are infrequent incidents among the thousands of reports issued every quarter.

More common are the efforts by companies to steer analysts' expectations with their own forecasts in the hope of avoiding surprises. SEC Regulation FD permits doing so as long as these forecasts are first made public.

This behavior has attracted the attention of some academic researchers. In an article written for the *Financial Analysts Journal*,[4] accounting professors Maribeth Collier and Teri Lombard Yohn summarized the findings of some of the research. Here is part of their summary:

1. Company forecasts are not systematically higher than existing analyst forecasts or than actual earnings.

2. Companies that forecast have greater percentage changes in earnings than nonforecasting firms, and greater percentage changes in earnings for the period being forecast relative to nonforecasting periods.

3. Analysts will respond to company forecasts, and their responses are greater when the forecast yields a surprise.

4. Surprise announcements tend to come from small companies.

It appears that there are no surprises when it comes to studying surprises. Why bother forecasting for the analysts? The real danger in this behavior is that it is a distraction from running the business. The result of that "misfocusing" might be some real surprises. Your inattention to operations could impede the company's progress. After all, you are the boss—or were.

The risk of making forecasts is too great for an emerging company, and was so before the enactment of Regulation FD. There is absolutely nothing that will repulse the pros more than being told something quite different than what you subsequently include in your 10-Q report. Your steering attempts will have compounded the consequences of some unexpected news.

Your best approach is to disclose, via a press release, any material change that could impact earnings and/or shareholder equity. The timing of the press release should be after you, and your financial staff, have agreed that there is a material change that will affect financial performance. The announcement should then be released before any other mention of the circumstances is disclosed to anyone.

Regulation FD mandates protection for investors, *not for companies*. Some companies have made the mistake of prematurely announcing to the public a new product, a new sales contract, or an R&D breakthrough that subsequently didn't work out. This can charitably be called enthusiastic behavior. It can uncharitably, and most usually, be called *stupid* behavior. Stay in the safe harbor. When in doubt about what you can disclose, KYMS (Keep Your Mouth Shut).

Our Advice (Besides KYMS)

You are correct if you have inferred that the authors advise against playing the forecasting earnings game. We tell our clients to conduct their IR activities based on what's right for shareholders over the long term. One CEO, frustrated about Wall Street's overemphasis of the short term, responded caustically, "We won't have any shareholders in the long term!" Our counter is that, sooner than later, intelligent people will realize that Wall Street can't price every stock, every day. Smart money gets smarter. We believe that overreaction leads to underreaction. The number of informed players in the U.S. equity markets continues to increase. Most importantly, a lot of players are pension managers with ever-nearing funding liabilities. We are betting *our business* that they will act and react to moderate consensus risk.

The companies with higher market caps than yours have an alternative that you don't. They can buy back some of their stock and wait. You have a float problem.

Hang in there with sound and prudent business practices. Revisit your plan and revise it accordingly. Meet the challenges you confront on Wall Street the same way you confront them in your own marketplace. Face the realities of public-company life, one of which will be that, for better or worse, the price of your stock approximates the intrinsic worth and the near-term prospects of your company.

Chapters 7 and 8 focus exclusively on the compliance and suggested best practices of financial reporting. The number of individuals owning stocks directly, or through intermediaries, continues to increase. The regulators, the media, investor groups, and fiduciaries are becoming increasingly vigilant about what represents appropriate accounting and classification of revenues and expenses. There are thousands of companies in which they can invest. Why risk investing in a company whose financial reporting is dubious?

At this point, some readers could be disappointed that we haven't prescribed any surefire and easily implemented solutions to the challenges inherent in consensus risk. We don't know any.

INDEPENDENT INVESTMENT MANAGERS

In addition to the managers of microcap growth mutual funds, there are several independent investment managers who specialize in stocks like those of your company. There are other independents that are not wed to an investment style. They will include microcap stocks in their investment mix for diversification and return enhancement. The total market values of these portfolios are usually less than $50 million. The practices and selection criteria of these managers are no different from what we have discussed.

FIDUCIARIES

Pension plan sponsors are responsible for overseeing billions of dollars. Investing in microcap securities won't have any impact on their funding, so they won't bother investing in them. Their impact on companies like yours is indirect, as we mentioned earlier. Their preponderance and attendant moral suasion should mitigate consensus risk.

Local pension plans, however, could have some interest in your company.

LOCAL INSTITUTIONAL INVESTORS

In addition to local pension plans, there is some evidence that large, and small, investment managers, of any style, should consider investing in local corporations. Some extensive research by Joshua Coval, of the University of Michigan, and Tobias Moskowitz, of the University of Chicago,[5] uncovered strong evidence that geographic proximity between a fund manager and an investment significantly influences returns. Their analysis of 1,200 U.S. funds and 4,600 companies between 1975 and 1994 prompted them to state, "[F]unds with the highest local bias exhibit larger gains from investing locally (2.07 percent per year)." Obviously, you don't call the local fund managers until you know their selection criteria. You shouldn't be surprised to discover that they probably know all about you.

Your close-to-home efforts, though, are best directed to unions, state and local foundations and endowments. Is there a place for your company's stock in the portfolio of your local college or hospital? Maybe the trust department at a local bank has a policy of carrying securities of regional or local companies. Do not overlook these institutional investors. Again, their practices and selection criteria won't differ from those we have discussed in this chapter.

OTHER PLAYERS

Stock price movements are affected by "players" other than portfolio managers and security analysts.

Brokers

What if you are a stockbroker? Uncertainty leads to herding. Herding can increase volume (up or down). Increased volume increases commissions. Commissions are good, so herding is good.

Technicians and Their Charts

There are some portfolio managers and analysts who do not rely on fundamental and accounting measures to value stocks. They focus on the direction of price changes and on changes in transaction volume. These market participants are known as *technicians, technical analysts, chartists,* and, to the academics, *momentum investors.* This group believes that by charting these patterns of changes they can forecast stock prices over the short term. Because of the light trading volume of stocks like those of your company, technicians have no interest in your company.

CONCLUSION

No public company will have a credible shareholder constituency without some institutional investors. Managers of microcap growth portfolios, and some independent money managers, are the institutional investors that will be interested in the stocks of emerging companies. Attracting microcap growth portfolio managers requires a deep understanding of their risk management practices as well as their selection criteria. An understanding of the environment in which they operate is also critical to attracting their investment. The actions, reactions, or inaction, of these atypical investment professionals are major factors affecting the market value of your company's stock.

NOTES

1. Wayne Wagner and Steven Glass, "Analyzing Transaction Costs: Part I," *The Journal of Investment Consulting* 1 (June 1999): 6.

2. Magnus Buchan, "The Profitability Dilemma," *Red Herring* (March 2000).

3. Russ Wermers, "Mutual Fund Herding and the Impact on Stock Prices," *The Journal of Finance* (April 1999).

4. Maribeth Collier and Teri Lombard Yohn, "Management Forecasts: What Do We Know?," *Financial Analysts Journal* (January/February 1998).

5. Joshua D. Coval and Tobias J. Moskowitz, "The Geography of Investment: Informed Trading and Asset Pricing," Center for Research in Securities Prices, University of Chicago, *Working Paper no. 502.*

CHAPTER 6

Reaching the Individual Investor

INDIVIDUAL INVESTORS BUY STOCK in small lots, are less sophisticated, and are the investors most likely to generate complaints. What, then, is the appeal of having a core of individual shareholders? They tend to hold their shares the longest; therefore, they create the most stable portion of your shareholder base. If your company demonstrates its ability to grow shareholder equity, they will be the first to buy more of your stock. A solid cadre of individual stockholders is evidence to brokers, traders, and institutions that your company's stock is a viable investment.

There are two ways of reaching new individual investors—directly and indirectly. Directly is the most problematic. The retail audience is broad, so it's more costly to reach. The cost can be prohibitive when it's computed on a per-buy basis.

THE RETAIL STOCKBROKER

Retail brokers provide a proven means of reaching individual investors. These brokers represent a leveraged use of your IR budget and activity. A broker provides an opportunity to tell your story once and have it repeated scores of times. Moreover, brokers are your compliance "shield." They know securities law. They know what they can and cannot say. Brokers can insulate your company from disclosure problems.

Although institutions do make purchases in large lots of tens of thousands of shares, they don't do so with a large degree of frequency. If a broker is convinced that your stock's price represents value, he or she will be encouraging its purchase every trading day. Daily volume for emerging company stocks is created by retail brokers and their customers. Without this daily volume, you are less likely to attract the attention of institutional investors.

On occasion, when we sit down with clients, we are asked, "You must have 10 or 12 broker friends who will step in and start selling our stock, don't you?," the implication being, "if you are such a good IR firm, then you must have people that will follow your recommendations to the letter." If we have known 10 or 12 broker friends who sold stock to clients simply because we said so, we would have long since lost them as friends. The approach to working with brokers can't be "favor" based. One needs to be as deliberate and systematic in reaching them as in reaching institutional investors.

In Chapter 4 we advocate bypassing the broker/dealer research analysts and communicating directly with institutional investors. When we have proposed that strategy, many clients have responded with the legitimate concern that bypassing the analysts precludes reaching retail brokers. They have some knowledge of how major retail broker operations work and are concerned they will never be featured on a morning "squawk box."[1] They're correct, they won't. For the same reason we gave on page 31.

With respect to individual investors, you have to work with the sell side; however, we recommend going directly to "selected" brokers. Bypass the research and supervisory people. You select these brokers through a process of elimination similar to that proposed in Chapter 4 for targeting institutional money managers. Employing this winnowing process requires knowledge of the present state of the retail stockbroker industry.

Making the Cuts

One overriding fact about retail brokers is that their number is decreasing. Internet (brokerless) trading now accounts for nearly one-third of all securities transactions. For those who are surprised by this, there is confirmation. The *Red Book,* published by Standard and Poor's division of McGraw-Hill, is a compilation of all brokerage firms and their offices in the United States and Canada. Their listings have shrunk by more than half during the past five years.

The other overriding fact is the manner in which many of the existing brokers from the major firms now conduct their business. More than 25 percent of finance professionals dealing directly with individual investors don't earn commissions on stock transactions. Their compensation is based on fees earned on the amount of their clients' assets that they directed to professional money management enterprises, including mutual and hedge funds.[2] These investment professionals are commonly known as fee-based consultants, financial planners, or wrap-account brokers. This group is easily identified as candidates for your first cut.

You can eliminate, among the remaining commission (earning) groups, those who have had less than five years' experience working as a stockbroker. These neophytes will probably not have experienced any sustained down markets. They most likely won't be candidates with whom you can establish a sustained relationship. Even if there are, among this group, some brokers who have demonstrated potential for survival, they won't have earned the autonomy to make their own recommendations. They are still under the thumb of their branch manager, and their agenda may be reset everyday by the squawk box.

The next group of brokers who should be eliminated as candidates for promoting your company's stock are those brokers whose clients have low tolerances for risk. Demographics dictate that this is the largest subset of retail brokers (as the largest group of investors are more than 50 years old). This group of investors must carry the overriding concern of capital preservation. Keep in mind the disagreeable reality that the stock of your emerging company is perceived as a high-risk investment. Don't waste time trying to alter that perception.

Your Best Retail Prospects

The best target profile is a broker with 10 or more years of successful experience dealing with high-net-worth clients, preferably accredited investors.[3] These clients have usually designated some percentage of their investment capital for alternative investments. This category includes hedge funds, venture capital funds, leveraged buyout funds, IPOs, emerging growth stocks, and leveraged strategies involving options and futures contracts.

Yes, there are many retail brokers and financial planners who characterize your company's stock as an alternative investment.

There are also brokers who maintain a list of clients who have adopted a strategy of identifying and investing in the stocks of companies like yours. Even though these clients are willing to assume a higher level of risk, they cannot be characterized as gamblers or speculators. They are aware they could lose most of their investment in some companies, but they expect commensurate rewards on the stocks of other emerging firms. Moreover, these investors derive great pleasure from being part of a growing company.

The Worst Retail Prospects

Our investor-relations policy dictates that we avoid brokers who cater to speculators and gamblers—those who "flip stocks" or chase what we call "hot money." By hot-money chasers, we mean people who are hoping for a quick profit on their money, so that they can sell and go after the next "hot deal." This is impatient money, and it is gone within weeks.

"PUMP AND DUMP" AND OTHER CHICANERY

Hot money has no value for the emerging company with the deliberate goal of increasing shareholders' equity. One doesn't have to work very long with emerging companies' investor relations programs before encountering "financial advisors" who propose campaigns "guaranteed" to dramatically increase the price of a company's stock.

Benjamin Mark Cole, in his cogent book, *The Pied Pipers of Wall Street,* calls these "advisors" the "Pied Pipers with the Brass Flutes."[4] Companies like yours are in the crosshairs of these operators. You and your insiders should maintain constant vigilance against them.

On your worst days, you can be aggravated about the prospects for your company's stock. This state of mind can, understandably, make you susceptible to the pitch of some "Wall Street Pro" who has a surefire plan to dramatically increase the price of your company's stock.

The most common of these plans is a game often referred to as "pump and dump." Here is Cole's concise description of this scheme:

> *The pump-and-dump scheme is when a group of traders [and brokers] artificially boost the share price of a selected stock . . . and then sell out before reality hits and the [price of the] stock plummets. They usually do this by coordinating timed purchases with a wildly positive public relations campaign, the centerpiece of which is generally a highly favorable analyst's report — the enthusiastic analyst being a hired accomplice who is often paid in stock for his efforts.[5]*

As Cole points out, stocks of emerging companies, such as yours, are the targets. And one reason for this is their small floats. A small float is the cause of less liquidity, which translates into volatility. Cole further states, "As a result, even a small amount of buying 'pressure' — artificially induced or otherwise — can send small-cap stocks soaring. Then the 'pumpers' can dump."[6]

If you are approached by a broker (or analyst) with a plan to increase the price of your company's stock within a few weeks, be wary. Ask for the names and affiliations of those who will be working on "the campaign."

To check out a broker or brokerage house go to the NASD Web site—NASD.com. Follow the instructions and you will be able to find out whether a broker or brokerage house has had any problems with the NASD. This is the appropriate regulatory body for broker/dealer questions.

Pay particular attention to what the campaign proponent is focusing on with respect to your company. If that person is indifferent to the details of your business strategy, your cost controls, your competitive analysis, and the profiles of your customers, how sincere can that "Wall Street Pro" be about the long-term prospects for your company? Make a point to get the names of other companies that the "Pro" has worked with and call them. You cannot be too vigilant.

> **Once your company has been the subject of a pump-and-dump scheme, its reputation within the investment community has been besmirched—that is always the aftermath. Restoring the appeal of your company is most likely impossible.**

WEB CHAT ROOMS

Cyberspace offers unlimited creativity for the renegade broker and his or her associates. The problems associated with this activity are so extensive that we have devoted an entire chapter to the topic—Chapter 9.

THE LESS THAN GIFTED BROKER

The SEC explicitly prohibits any broker employed as such by a securities firm from accepting payment from a company in exchange for agreeing to make a market in that company's stock or for promoting a stock on the broker's own initiative. In addition to these practices being illegal, there is another reason to decline any such arrangement: Who would want to do business with a broker stupid enough to make such a proposal?

TARGETING THE BEST RETAIL BROKERS

The brokers we have profiled as targets have learned that real success is sustained success. The key to sustained success is retaining their clients. They work hard to recommend stocks that will make their clients money within each client's suitability. These brokers work carefully and deliberately; therefore, they don't jump at an initial presentation. The most successful brokers are those who select the securities they sell in the same manner as portfolio managers select the securities they buy.

Our target brokers work at big brokerage firms and small firms. Where they work dictates, in some respects, *how* they work, and what they are allowed to do.

Megafirm Brokers

Megafirms are the full-service broker/dealers with extensive research and investment banking divisions. They have offices throughout the world. Their research divisions employ scores of analysts who cover a large number of securities throughout many sectors. The primary focus of research by these analysts are companies with market capitalizations of more than $1 billion. These firms generally have policies that prevent their brokers from performing transactions involving stocks priced below $5 a share. These firms have a large overhead of administrative costs. They must have high commission and fee revenues in order to operate profitably. Transactions in higher-priced shares will naturally generate higher commissions.

Regional Brokers

Regional firms are full-service broker/dealers that generally do not have a national presence. They usually have a multi-state presence. They are most likely to require their brokers to operate under strictures similar to those faced by megafirm brokers. They structure their operations in a manner that discourages low-revenue transactions. Their distinctive appeal is that they may have some brokers who do specialize in stocks of emerging companies within their region. Their aim of having a few brokers focusing on companies like yours is to cultivate a relationship from which will evolve investment-banking business.

Independent Brokers

There exist throughout the country brokerage firms that are independently owned. These firms employ just a few brokers (as few as 5, as many as 100) who are supervised by the owner of the firm. The NASD requires a qualified supervisory principal to be present at any brokerage office during trading hours. In compliance with this stricture, brokers at these firms have most likely met all the licensing requirements necessary to become a supervising principal in a broker/dealer. These brokers don't enjoy the degree of autonomy that one might expect. Because they are easy to find and their transactions easy to monitor and audit, these firms find themselves subject to close scrutiny by state and federal regulators. They are less likely to be involved in any chicanery.

Microcap Brokers

There may be an experienced broker in the offices of any size firm (mega, regional, or independent) who has established a good track record with microcap stocks. A good track record is a history of generating commissions that are higher than the mean among all the firm's brokers. Those brokers most likely will have at least 10 years of experience and have client lists mostly comprising accredited investors. These brokers' track records allow them some autonomy in stock selection. They typically do their own research. They will often begin their search for appropriate companies within the communities where they work. They may be familiar with your company. If you are contacted by local brokers, make time to talk with them. These brokers will want to visit and observe your company's operations. During the visit, be alert to the disclosure strictures.

Don't provide any information that has not been disclosed publicly with regard to future revenue and earnings. You are free to talk about your competitive advantage, your plans for growth, and your cost-control process. Be careful that neither you nor anyone else on site talks about anything specific to revenues, order backlogs, new products, or new services unless that information has been published.

It is very time consuming to determine whether there are brokers in your area that specialize in emerging growth companies. We suggest delegating the initial search to an administrative assistant. Give the assistant the telephone numbers of those regional branch offices within an hour's drive from your company's locations. When calling an office, the assistant should ask to speak to the branch manager. These calls should always be made before the opening of trading on the New York Stock Exchange or after the close (9:30 A.M. eastern time to 4:00 P.M. eastern time). Instruct the caller to ask the branch manager, "Is there any broker on your staff that specializes in small, emerging companies?" If so, your assistant should get the brokers' names and direct-dial numbers and give them to you or some senior-level manager for follow-up.

The same process of winnowing brokers can be adapted to reach brokers across the country, but first you need lists of distant brokers to winnow. There are available lists of brokers who specialize in serving accredited investors. An obvious source for the names are your high-net-worth acquaintances across the country. It is onerous and time consuming to build a list of stockbrokers who then must be qualified further by asking them if they recommend selected microcap stocks to their clients. We trust that you aren't dismayed at our suggesting an alternative approach, which is to retain an experienced investor relations firm that has already made an investment in developing a list of qualified stockbrokers.

COMMUNICATING WITH BROKERS

Whatever messages your company intends to send to its corps of selected brokers, the messages must always be in this context: *How is this meaningful to the owners and potential owners of the company's stock? How will it affect the market value of the company's stock?*

Using the Telephone

Brokers are accustomed to dealing with people over the phone. Most of their transactions are conducted over the phone. When you have brokers on the phone who say that they do have clients who invest in companies like yours, you already have their attention. Ask the broker if this is an appropriate time to discuss your company. If it is not, make an appointment to call the broker back. Willingness to have you call back is a strong expression of interest. When you have the broker's attention, on the initial call, or the call back, be concise. Give the name of your company and its listing symbol. Then describe your product or service in no more than two sentences. Explain who your intended customers are. Avoid industry jargon and complicated technical concepts. Tell how long you have been in business and then shut up. Let the broker ask the questions. Remember, don't disclose any information that has not been made public. Offer to send more information and refer the broker to your Web site. Give the dates of your most recent 10-Q and 10-K filings.

Printed Material

If the broker accepts your offer for information other than what the broker can obtain from your Web site and EDGAR, send the broker one or both of two information pieces that you keep in stock and updated. The first item is a one-page fact sheet containing 8 to 10 bulleted items that speak to the question: Why should anyone be interested in your company? An example is included in Chapter 11.

The second printed piece is an executive summary with a format similar to a research report. Again, an example is included in Chapter 11. See Appendix 11–A.

Don't send copies of a Power Point presentation. They are of little value without an accompanying narrative.

That Matter of Follow-Up

The real challenge to building an individual investor relations program is sustaining the relationship with retail brokers. Always keep in mind that you are competing with thousands of other public companies vying for stockbrokers' attention. Don't ever assume that the brokers with whom you have relationships will stay abreast of your company's activities on their own initiative. You must have a system in place that ensures these valuable people are in the "immediate need to know" loop about events and circumstances that affect the price of your company's stock. Chapter 12 has suggestions on establishing and administering such a system.

The Direct Approach

We advise against conducting any campaign whereby you, or members of your company, promote your stock directly to new individual investors. You run several risks. The most serious is that you may lose the services of the brokers. One service of the retail brokers is that of filtering out the inappropriate investor. There are some classes of investors who may not share your goal of building an enduring company. These classes may be inadvertently solicited through your company's campaign. Second, shareholders acquired directly are the most likely to come directly to you for information and reports rather than receiving it from their broker. This can create an unnecessary workload on valued staff. Another important reason is that by directly soliciting purchases of your stock, you could be in violation of one of the hundreds of state, federal, and exchange rules that govern securities transactions.

The basic tenet of investor relations and investor recruitment is that *all the activities of the company are supposed to be directed to enhancing investment appeal.* This means your sales, your marketing, your advertising, the quality of your product or service, your customer service, and your reputation. You and your employees should be occupied and preoccupied with these challenges.

The only action that you or members of your company should personally take toward soliciting new investors is to include in your advertising and press releases the fact that you are a public company. List where your stock trades and include your trading symbol(s).

RESEARCH, THE QUID PRO QUO

In Chapter 4 we advise against approaching the sell side research analyst. There may be instances when one of the brokers you have cultivated will refer an analyst from his or her firm to you. In that instance, you should work with that analyst. Just remember that you are a source of new business for the firm. In addition to asking for your investment banking business, don't be surprised if the firm offers to run your employee stock ownership plan (ESOP), profit sharing plan, and 401(k) plan. How about handling your insider transactions and providing discount brokerage services? When, not if, these services are proposed, we suggest you respond: "Thank you. We will give these offers serious consideration, if you agree to be one of our retail market makers." Don't agree to any arrangement to manage your ESOP or retirement programs without first clearing the arrangement with counsel. Federal regulations prohibit certain "related party" agreements between brokers and plan-sponsoring companies.

Fees for Research

Emerging companies seeking Nasdaq or exchange listings are asked by regulators if they have paid for research. This question is intended to determine whether you have made direct cash payments (hard dollars) to a newsletter or Web site. There is nothing illegal about this transaction *providing the publisher of the research discloses that they have been paid for the report.* The disclosure generally appears at the end of the research report. Regulators have been studying this area.

The reality is that research has always been paid for with investment banking and commission fees, hard dollars, or newsletter subscriptions. In our discussion with some regulators about this matter, they do admit to some concern about the extent of disclosing payments for research, directly or indirectly. Investment firms are now required to post a disclaimer on a report that they have a business relationship with the subject of the research.

CONCLUSION

A base of individual investors is necessary to provide your company's stock with liquidity and a stable trading range. The time involved to cultivate and recruit appropriate retail stockbrokers is a necessary investment. This cadre of brokers can be one of your best lines of defense when economic events or a poor quarter depresses stock prices.

NOTES

1. The squawk box is a speakerphone connected to branch offices of a major brokerage firm. These devices are used at regular intervals and sporadically throughout the day in order to update the entire sales force. Most firms sponsor a morning call prior to the market open. They give their opinions for the short-, intermediate-, and long-term market conditions. They also share new research or information that might be pertinent to the current market.

2. As the discerning reader has already concluded, there might be some IR opportunity among the fee-based brokers. The authors know two wrap-account brokers who include microcap growth managers among their list of recommended portfolios. These microcap managers will make time to meet with us, because we were referred by a broker who is promoting that manager's fund.

3. An accredited or "qualified" investor is generally considered to be an individual with an annual income of at least $250,000, and liquid assets of at least $1 million.

4. Benjamin Mark Cole, *The Pied Pipers of Wall Street* (Princeton, NJ: Bloomberg Press, 2001), 132.

5. Ibid.

6. Ibid.

Compliance and Disclosure

CHAPTER 7

Financial Reporting

LYNN TURNER, CHIEF ACCOUNTANT of the Securities Exchange Commission, addressed the Colorado Association of CPAs on December 15, 2000. Among his remarks was this one:

> Today, over 80 million investors participate in [the U.S. capital] markets, providing over 15,000 companies a source of capital, and generating approximately $16 trillion in wealth for investors. And this success is in no small part due to the trust and confidence the investing public place in the financial information they receive and analyze.

The foregoing was delivered sincerely and with conviction, and has been so delivered by other Securities and Exchange Commission (SEC) staff across the country for many years. Sincerity and conviction, backed up with a commitment to strict enforcement. Your public company *will* provide financial information that the SEC believes is worthy of *its* "trust and confidence." Make no mistake. The SEC is watching how your public company keeps its books. If persons in your emerging company recommend some chicanery in your financial reporting process, suggest that those people consult a qualified mental health professional. Do this while you are helping them clean out their desks.

THE SECURITIES AND EXCHANGE COMMISSION (SEC)

The SEC is a federal agency, established by the Securities Exchange Act of 1934. The '34 Act is a keystone in the regulation of securities markets. It outlines the powers of the SEC to interpret, supervise, and enforce the securities laws of the United States, principally those prohibiting fraud. The SEC has the authority to bring administrative proceedings against firms and persons the agency believes are violating securities laws; however, allegations of criminal violations of the laws are prosecuted by the Justice Department. The Justice Department takes very seriously such allegations by the SEC. The functions of the SEC can be considered quasi-judicial in nature, because appeals from its decisions can be taken to federal courts of appeals. Figure 7–1 is an organization chart of the SEC.

The SEC and Financial Reporting

Ensuring full and fair disclosure of all material facts about companies whose securities are publicly traded is one of the SEC's major responsibilities. The SEC's Division of Corporate Finance ensures that information contained in new issue prospectuses and IPO offerings (red herrings) is complete and not misleading. The Office of the Chief Accountant deals with matters relating to financial reporting. *Regulation S-X* governs the form and content of financial statements and the means by which financial information is reported to the SEC. The agency, from time to time, issues documents that detail and update its reporting prescriptions and recommendations. Two of the most frequent issues are the accounting series releases (ASRs) and the financial reporting releases (FRRs).

FIGURE 7-1   U.S. Securities and Exchange Commission

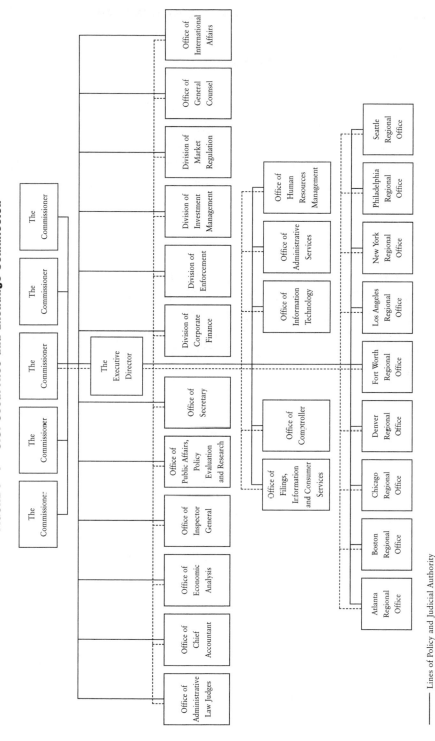

— Lines of Policy and Judicial Authority

----- Lines of Budget and Management Authority

SEC Financial Filing Requirements

The Commission requires your company to file a number of specific reports with it. Table 7–1 is a listing of the reports most frequently filed and the information that must be included in each. The most common reports are the 10-K and the 10-Q. The financial statements and any accompanying notes disclosed in the 10-K are required to have been reviewed and accepted by an outside independent auditor. The 10-K must be filed with the SEC within 90 days after the end of your company's fiscal year. 10-Q statements are filed quarterly within 45 days from the end of each fiscal quarter.

The 8-K report must be filed *WHEN YOUR COMPANY UNDERGOES SOME IMPORTANT EVENT THAT YOUR STOCK-HOLDERS SHOULD KNOW ABOUT.*

Investors can retrieve and review most SEC reports on the SEC Web site *(www.sec.gov)* under EDGAR (Electronic Data Gathering and Retrieval).

The SEC and the Auditing Process

In the Denver speech cited above, Lynn Turner turned the focus to the auditing of a firm's financial reporting:

> *[I]t takes all three pillars of financial reporting, the financial executive, the independent auditor, and the audit committee [of the board of directors], to maintain the foundation upon which the success of our markets have [sic] been built.*

Chief Financial Officer

In Turner's words, the "responsibility for the numbers rests squarely on the shoulders of the CFO. It is this person in your company who must establish and monitor the internal controls necessary to provide reasonable assurance that the financial statements have been prepared in accordance with generally accepted accounting principles."

TABLE 7–1 What Should Be Included in SEC Filings 10-K, 10-Q, and 8-K

A–Always Included, F–Frequently Included

Report Contents	10-K	10-Q	8-K
Auditor Name	A		
Auditor Opinion	A		
Auditor Changes			A
Nature of Business	A		
History of Business	F		
Changes in Organization	A		A
Debt Structure	A		
Depreciation Schedules	A		
Dilution Factors	A		A
Directors, Officers, and Insiders	A		
Earnings per Share	A	A	
Annual Audited Financial Information	A		
Interim Unaudited Financial Information		A	A
Foreign Operations	A		
Legal Agreements	F		
Loan Agreements	F	F	
Plants and Properties	A		
Products and Services	A		
Securities Structures	A	F	
Subsidiaries	A	A	
Major Changes in Shareholders	A	A	A

Turner left no doubt about the extent of his concerns with respect to spurious press releases:

> *These releases put a spin on the numbers that seem to turn straw into gold. They reflect "pro-forma" numbers at the beginning of the release that set forth profits after basic expenses have been added back, such as costs for marketing or for starting up a new product line. Or the company gave ongoing profits a boost by adding in one-time recurring gains without explanation. I have also seen items added that clearly do not comply with the Commission's Regulation S-X. . . . [W]e will continue to urge investors to be cautious and read the entire interim and annual reports filed with the Commission.*

In the Denver speech, the Chief Accountant had no trouble keeping his audience's attention. In discussing the recently issued report from the Panel on Audit Effectiveness (see *www.pobauditpanel. org*), and the CFO's role in ensuring creditable audits, Turner shifted the context to that of indictment and sentencing:

> *[D]ata shows that the average prison sentence from SEC referrals to U.S. Attorney's offices is growing longer, from 10 months in 1992 to 49 months in 1998. And with creation of the SEC's Financial Fraud Task Force this year, I suspect the number of referrals may increase. As Richard Walker, the SEC's Enforcement Division Director, has stated, "We are moving towards turning the numbers game into a game of Monopoly." That is, cook the books and you will go directly to jail without passing Go.*

Seven months later in the July 6, 2001, issue of *The Wall Street Journal,* Walker was quoted, "If we had nothing else to do, the accounting investigations alone would keep us busy for the next five to ten years." In the same article, Turner announced that the SEC's goal for the fiscal year ending September 30, 2001, was to review one out of every four 10-Ks filed.

Board of Directors Audit Committee

Your audit committee should be composed of outside, independent directors. Listen to Turner about the importance of your audit committee. "We will continue to ask audit committees to play a more active role to ensure investors receive a balanced, complete, transparent picture of the company's financial condition and results. And I have every faith that audit committees will do just that." Not underestimating the intelligence of the audience, Turner didn't talk about the consequences of not living up to the faith expressed.

See Appendix 7–A for sample audit committee charter.

Independent Auditor

Form 10-K must be prepared and audited under the scrutiny of a qualified, outside accounting firm. The SEC is appropriately obsessive about your company's efforts to ensure the auditor's independence from any influence exerted by someone from your company, *or by someone from the auditor's firm*. The concern about influence exerted from within the auditor's firm has evolved from the way the large multi-national accounting firms have transformed themselves. These huge firms have established consulting practices in information management, benefits administration, and strategic planning, the revenues from which match or exceed those from their traditional business accounting and tax form preparation.

The SEC's appropriate concern is conflict of interest. How impartial is the audit certification from a firm that is also receiving significant revenues for consulting services rendered? An emerging company probably won't be engaging a "Big Five" firm as its outside auditor; however, smaller CPA firms seeking to do business with your company may offer other services, such as managing your benefits program or advising about complying with state and federal employment laws. You can be confronted with a conflict of interest situation.

Chief Accountant Turner strongly recommends that your company use a 10-factor list developed by the O'Malley Commission for "reasoned guidance" in determining an outside auditor's independence (see *www.pobauditpanel.org*).

Private-Sector Dictates

Adherence to and compliance with SEC reporting requirements are prerequisites for Nasdaq and exchange listings. Even though the SEC oversees and dictates its own rules and procedures, it actively encourages the private sector to develop generally accepted accounting practices (GAAP). The private-sector organization recognized as the standard setter for GAAP is the Financial Accounting Standards Board (FASB).

FINANCIAL ACCOUNTING STANDARDS BOARD (FASB).   FASB is the authoritative *U.S.* standard setter for GAAP. FASB standards are not necessarily adhered to by countries incorporated outside the United States; however, if they want their stocks, American Depositary Receipts, or Safe Custody Receipts (ADRs/SDRs) listed in the United States, they must adhere to FASB standards.

The FASB standards are officially recognized as authoritative by the SEC and by the American Institute of Certified Professional Accountants (AICPA). FASB was established in 1973 as the successor to the much-criticized Accounting Principles Board (APB).

ELEMENTS OF EFFECTIVE FINANCIAL REPORTING

In Chapter 5, we briefly discuss how microcap investment managers analyze your financial reports (see pages 44 – 47). Our goal was to make you aware that these investment professionals assigned greater weight to different measures depending on their approaches to measuring operating efficiencies. Even though they make relative judgments among all that data, do not infer that they regard any of it as unimportant. What is presented in the income statement, the balance sheet, and the statement of cash flows is pertinent and relevant to everyone in that shareholder constituency you are working to build.

Hear what a portfolio manager with more than $5 billion under management told members of the National Investor Relations Institute (NIRI):

> "We slice and dice every possible number. Before, a company would hit its earnings mark and everything was fine." The onus is on investor relations people to be able "to address every angle of the business and financials, and answer every question of interest to investors." And keep in mind that the Chief Accountant is urging investors, ". . . to read the entire interim and annual report filed with the Commission."

Income Statement

The income statement reports earnings, about which there are two concerns. Can an increase in earnings be sustained, and how were the earnings computed? We have addressed the implications with respect to the first question in our discussion of consensus risk (see pages 48–53). The second question provides the focus for what follows.

Revenues

In 2000, FASB issued new revenue recognition rules, most notably mandating distinctions between gross revenues and net revenues. *Gross revenue* is the amount invoiced. *Net revenue* is how much the company retains after paying a wholesaler or manufacturer for the invoiced products. The experienced investor recognizes this as a cost of goods sold (COGS) issue. Past practice for "old economy" firms was to report in their gross income computations a deduction of the direct (actual) COGS. Several microcap companies within the technology and biotech sectors were computing otherwise. How was this permissible?

The question of permissibility has been succinctly treated in an excellent article by Julia Lawlor in the December 4, 2000, issue of *Red Herring*.[1] Many E-merchants operate as agents, rather than principals, in a transaction. There have been no bricks-and-mortar travel agencies who ever booked as revenue the costs to its customers of the travel and lodging the agencies reserved.

They booked the commissions. Priceline.com booked as revenue the full price of the reservation it arranged for a customer. Lawlor cites the Priceline.com dubious justification: "[A]lthough it doesn't take title to the product until after the customer has made a nonrefundable purchase by credit card, it assumes the risk if the customer's credit is bad, the charge is disputed, or the supplier goes out of business." The diligent investor understands that "disputed" is the only operative word in that rationale.

Lawlor also addresses the practices among merging biotech firms:

> *Historically, biotech companies have gotten up front fees when they have affiliated with big pharmaceutical companies for joint research and development arrangements. These fees are booked immediately as revenue, under the assumption that the payment is for research the company has already completed. But the SEC says the payments should be spread over the term of the agreement.*

Resist the temptation to smooth out lumpy revenues. The SEC and the money managers look upon revenue smoothing as misrepresentation. Delays in posting revenue do occur, and informed professionals understand this. What they don't like is to see the revenues from a larger than usual sale apportioned over several quarters. They are also concerned about the flip side of the revenue-posting issue: reporting all the revenue stipulated in a long-term contract as revenue received in one quarter.

The SEC's position is "revenue is recognized when it is earned and realized or realizable." The SEC describes four underlying positions that must exist:

1. There must be persuasive evidence that an arrangement exists.

2. Delivery of goods must have occurred or services must have been rendered.

3. The price is required to be fixed or determinable.

4. Collectibility is reasonably assured.

The key questions remain. Did money come in to the company as the result of a sale? Is any money owed to the actual selling *principal* in the transaction? Did you put that money into the operating account at the bank? Should some of the money have gone into a reserve account?

There is confusion about how to account for and report revenue transactions from strategic alliances, joint ventures, cross-licensing, and cross-ownership.

In discussing these revenue issues, Chief Accountant Turner remarked, "I would encourage registrants, [reporting companies], to consider discussing such highly unusual and complex transactions with the [SEC] staff on a pre-filing basis."

Expenses

The accrual questions about what should be charged as direct expenses and what should be capitalized are common to any listed company. These concerns have been around as long as there have been federal agencies. Consider how expenses are viewed from the perspective of the IRS and then from the perspective of the SEC. The perspective of the experienced investment manager is best represented with a quotation from one with more than 15 years' experience:

> *The accounting practices of the stocks we buy must portray economic reality, because economic reality is going to catch up with them one way or the other. One measure of economic reality is having expenses match up with the revenues they*

generate, whether those outlays are expensed or capitalized. There should be a good reason if they don't do so. Otherwise that company is a stock to avoid.

The SEC and FASB recognize that there is some incongruity with respect to accruals. That incongruity is the focus of dialogue on the campuses of some of the leading business schools. One of the scholars who is continually addressing accounting incongruities in his teaching, writing, and research is Baruch Lev at New York University's Stern School of Business. Lev argues that traditional accounting methods do not accurately *account* for intangibles such as R & D, innovation, brand positioning, or employee training. Lev's point is that like the purchase of machinery, these expenditures are investments, not expenses.

Lev was the subject of an extensive article by Jonathan R. Laing in the November 20, 2000, issue of *BARRON'S*.[2] We recommend this article as a point of departure for your own reflection about how these issues impact your company's reporting practices.

Balance Sheet

Face this fact. At some point in the early life of your company, the balance sheet should reflect a march to value. If you have been operating as a public company for more than five years, you should have an overall ratio of at least one and a quarter the amount of assets to liabilities. The experienced investors want an increase in their equity. They want you to have an increasing amount of cash or cash equivalents. When they look at your assets, they will pay particular attention to how you are accounting for your accounts receivable. How are you disclosing the provisions of your long-term and convertible debt? Are you disclosing conversion terms, call provisions, and balloon schedules at the end of the footnotes?

One entry on some balance sheets that remains forever aggravating is *goodwill* amortization. Goodwill is the difference between the purchase price paid for an acquisition and the fair value of the acquired company's assets. The arguments about goodwill are part of a larger dialogue about pooling-of-interests accounting. The criticism about this accounting method is that assets as well as earnings are overstated. Investment bankers and some companies counter that many mergers or acquisitions would not be approved by shareholders, because without the pooling of interests, the operating numbers would be significantly reduced.

The SEC, FASB, accounting firms, and academics cannot agree about how to resolve their disagreements. Your CFO, your audit committee, and your independent auditor must be in unanimous accord about how you will account for an acquisition and how you derive an amortization schedule related to the costs of that acquisition.

Statement of Cash Flows

Since 1988, the statement of cash flows has been the third form of financial reporting required to be filed. This is the "you can run, but you can't hide" report. There are no accruals here. There are three main sections in this report:

1. Cash flows from operations.
2. Cash flows from investing activities.
3. Cash flows from financing activities.

This is the statement experienced investors use to compute the net increase or decrease in your cash flow within the reporting period, and your company's *free cash flow*. Free cash flow is the money generated beyond your company's operating, financing, and investing needs. There will be, of course, a relationship between free cash flow and your liquid assets. Your emerging company may not have a free cash flow. You and your directors should agree that this is a condition to aspire for.

"Free" cash flow is not necessarily computed from any cash flow resulting from the tax reductions allowed from employees' exercising stock options. The practice of stock options continues to create financial reporting dilemmas.

Accounting for Options

The SEC, FASB, and shareholder advocacy groups continue issuing pronouncements, directives, and opinions about accounting for options. Ignore all comments about options' diluting stock values. This dialogue is not relevant to the valuation of your emerging company. Direct your attention to what is said about reporting in financial statements and proxies. Especially pertinent are matters dealing with valuation models and anything about the repricing of options.

Audit Fees

Your company is now required to report how much you paid annually to outside auditing firms. You're required to report how much was paid for nonaudit services to those auditing firms. This audit fee breakout is not a financial reporting activity. It is one of several *disclosure requirements,* which are the subject of the next chapter.

"Additional and Enhanced Information"

Early in the Denver talk, Chief Accountant Turner remarked:

> *I personally believe it is now time we find a way to provide investors with additional and enhanced information that will give investors greater predictive capabilities regarding the performance of the businesses they have chosen to invest in. A possible approach to accomplishing this would be for a company to choose ten to twelve key performance indicators, and disclose this information to investors in a consistent, comparable fashion. The company would be the party who chooses the indicators to be disclosed.*

Some scholars and accounting professionals have been in accord with this belief for some while. Professor Lev, Carolyn Brancato of

The Conference Board, Robert G. Eccles of Advisory Capital Partners, Inc., Harold Kahn of Scudder, Kemper Investments, Robert H. Herz of PricewaterhouseCoopers (PwC), and the Cap Gemini Ernst & Young Center for Business Innovation have been at the forefront of the argument that traditional accounting doesn't adequately reflect the real value of a publicly traded company. Eccles and Herz have co-authored a watershed book, *The ValueReporting Revolution* (John Wiley & Sons, 2001) with Herz's PwC colleagues E. Mary Keegan and David M.H. Phillips. In this book, the authors identify and categorize dozens of characteristics and performance measures that create value in a company yet are not "on the books." Research by Eccles and PwC provides evidence of a *direct link between revenues from new products and market-cap growth.*

We believe that there are investors who outperform the stock market. We believe that their sustained success is due to how they analyze companies. Winning investors have always looked beyond the numbers in the mandated reports. You and your management team should think about what you would add to your report if your company decided to implement the recommendations of Turner, Eccles, and the others. You will then be prepared to talk about them when they're raised in an interview with a savvy microcap portfolio manager.

NOTES

1. Julia Lawlor, "Book Cookery," *Red Herring,* December 4, 2000.
2. Jonathan R. Laing, "The New Math," *BARRON'S,* November 20, 2000.

Charter of the Audit Committee of the Board of Directors of The Boeing Company
(as amended May 1, 2000)

Although Boeing is a giant international company, we think this chapter is an excellent point of departure for developing an audit committee policy. It is reprinted with the permission of The Boeing Company.

ORGANIZATION

Members

The Audit Committee shall consist of three or more directors who are not members of the management and meet the independence and expertise requirements as defined by the New York Stock Exchange (NYSE) Listed Company Manual. The chairperson and members of the Committee shall be appointed by the Board of Directors at the annual organization meeting of the Board.

Meetings

Audit Committee meetings shall be in conjunction with regular Board of Directors meetings and at such other times as called by or on behalf of the chairperson of the Committee.

A majority of the members of the Audit Committee shall constitute a quorum. The Committee shall act only on the affirmative vote of at least two of the members.

ROLES

The function of the Audit Committee is oversight. In fulfilling their responsibilities hereunder, it is recognized that the members of the Audit Committee are not full-time employees of the Company and are not, and do not represent themselves to be, accountants or auditors by profession. As such, it is not the duty of the Audit Committee or its members to conduct "fieldwork" or other types of auditing or accounting reviews or procedures, and each member of the Audit Committee shall be entitled to rely on (i) the judgment of those persons and organizations within and outside the Company that it receives information from and (ii) the accuracy of the financial and other information provided to the Audit Committee by such persons or organizations.

RESPONSIBILITIES

The responsibilities of the Audit Committee are to:

1. Evaluate and select the outside auditor subject to ratification by the Board of Directors.

2. Review and advise on the selection and removal of the General Auditor. Additionally, the Audit Committee will review and recommend changes to the Internal Audit Charter.

3. Review, on an annual basis, a formal written statement prepared by the external auditor delineating all relationships relevant to audit independence between the auditor and the Company. This includes discussion of such relationships, and recommending that the Board of Directors take appropriate action in response to the outside auditor's report to satisfy itself of the outside auditor's independence.

4. Discuss with management or the independent auditor, as appropriate, the matters required to be discussed by Statement on Auditing Standards No. 61 relating to the conduct of the audit or quarterly review. This includes:

- Independent auditor responsibility under generally accepted auditing standards.

- Significant accounting policies.

- Management judgments and accounting estimates.

- Audit adjustments.

- Report on Form 10-K and other information in the Annual Report.

- Disagreements with management.

- Difficulties encountered in performing the audit.

- Consultations with other accountants.

- Major issues discussed with management prior to retention.

- Auditor's judgment about the quality of the entity's accounting principles.

5. Review with the independent auditors and members of senior management the adequacy and effectiveness of the Company's financial controls and financial reporting processes.

6. Meet at least annually with the senior internal auditing executive and the independent auditors in separate executive sessions.

7. Review, prior to filing, the Company's quarterly and annual reports filed with the Securities and Exchange Commission (SEC) on SEC Forms 10-Q and 10-K, including the Report of Management and Management's Discussion and Analysis in the Company's periodic reports to shareholders.

8. Prepare a report for inclusion in the annual proxy statement. The report will include at least the following:

- A statement that the Committee has reviewed and discussed the audited financial statements with management.

- A statement that the Committee has discussed with the independent auditors the matters required by Statement on Auditing Standards No. 61, *Required Communications with Audit Committees.*

- A statement that the Committee has reviewed written disclosures from, and held discussions with, the independent auditors on matters required by Independence Standards Board Statement No. 1, *Independence Discussions with Audit Committees.*

- A conclusion as to the Committee's Recommendation to the Board of Directors as to the filing of the Annual Report on Form 10-K with the Securities and Exchange Commission.

9. Review this charter on an annual basis and recommend to the Board of Directors changes to the charter as appropriate to support an affirmation by the Board of Directors.

10. Review management's assessment of compliance with laws, regulations, and Company policies relative to payments to individuals or organizations retained as foreign sales consultants.

11. Meet with representatives of the Board-appointed Ethics and Business Conduct Committee to review the Company's ethics and business conduct program and Company compliance with the principles of the Defense Industry Initiative on Business Ethics and Conduct.

12. Review significant pending and threatened litigation, the status of advancement of expenses to employees involved in company-related legal proceedings, and related indemnification.

13. Present to the Board of Directors such comments and recommendations as the Audit Committee deems appropriate, and perform such other duties as may be assigned by the Board or deemed appropriate by the Committee within the context of this charter.

CHAPTER 8

The Disclosure Challenge

THE MAJOR DIFFERENCE between a private company and a public company is the degree of regulatory compliance required. Complying with the regulations and practices governing the disclosure of *material* information is one of your biggest challenges. The disclosure challenge can be compounded by the imprecise notion of *materiality.*

Please note that required disclosures occur in two contexts. First, there are public disclosures in SEC reports or SEC registration statements. These disclosures must satisfy specific requirements of the SEC. The second context is sometimes referred to as informal disclosures. Disclosures are made in press releases and other broadly disseminated materials, particularly for current developments. All disclosures are subject to the general antifraud requirement (of SEC Rule 10b-5 under Section 10(b) of the Securities Exchange Act of 1934) that there be no untrue statement of material fact or misleading omission of a material fact. There are other rules that apply to statements to outside parties, and the discussion on Regulation FD (Reg. FD) is limited to this area.

The requirement of no trading with material, nonpublic information is also governed by this same general antifraud requirement.

This area has been developed by case law only until the recent addition of two new rules under Section 10(b) of the Securities Exchange Act of 1934.

MATERIALITY

The notion of materiality is imprecise, because governing bodies are reluctant to establish firm rules about determining materiality. The position of the Financial Accounting Standards Board (FASB) is "No general standards of materiality could be formulated to take into account all the considerations that enter into an experienced human judgment."

In October 2000, the SEC instituted Regulation FD (Fair Disclosure). Reg. FD requires public companies to disclose non-public, material information to all existing and potential investors if the information is disclosed to securities market professionals (such as broker/dealers, investment advisers, institutional investment managers, investment companies, hedge funds, and persons affiliated with the above) or holders of the company's securities who may be reasonably expected to trade on the basis of the information. In the language of Reg. FD, the SEC did not try to define *material* or *nonpublic*. We will discuss "nonpublic" later in the section dealing specifically with Reg. FD.

Regarding "material," the SEC deferred to some definitions established in case law. The general consensus of these definitions is that information is material "when there is a substantial likelihood that a reasonable shareholder would consider it important, and that the information would have been viewed by the reasonable shareholder as having significantly altered the total mix of information made available."

There are obvious events and information that "a reasonable investor would consider important," because those events or that information would have "significantly altered the total mix of information available":

- Change in earnings.
- Significant change in shareholder equity.

- Merger or acquisition.
- Joint venture.
- Tender offer.
- Changes in control or management.
- Changes in an audit or a change of auditors.
- New products or services.
- Issue regarding your capital structure (splits, etc.).

Thus, there is currently a vague, imprecise determination about what is material. The court or jury will decide what is important to a reasonable investor. Sometimes it can be difficult to ascertain materiality in context. For example, new products or services may be clearly material to you, yet that doesn't mean that all of them will be material to someone interested in your company. So with respect to materiality in the context of your business, our advice is to ask yourself

If some information about my company is omitted or mis-stated, will that omission or misstatement change the way investors value my company?

If the answer is yes, then that information should be considered material. You and your management team must always think about what is of significance and of consequence to investors who own or are thinking of owning stock in your company. When in doubt, a matter should be considered material.

REGULATION FD (FAIR DISCLOSURE)

In regard to whether information is "nonpublic" for purposes of Reg. FD, it's nonpublic if it has not been disseminated in a manner making it available to investors generally. Materiality is an issue of "what." "When" is the question begged by the nonpublic issue and to a lesser extent, the question of "how?" When and how have emerged as the keywords characterizing disclosure practices and policies because of the SEC's implementation of Reg. FD in October 2000.

Reg. FD was a response, in part, to the practice of sell side analysts sharing with selected institutional investors information that had been told to them by companies before the analysts disseminated their findings to the public at large. The SEC felt strongly that this practice put the individual investor at a disadvantage. This practice of *selective disclosure* was so pervasive within broker/dealer research firms and among large public companies that the SEC felt it had to be curbed. Otherwise, they reasoned, investors would lose faith and confidence in the fairness and transparency of the securities markets. The direct quotation from one of the SEC's press releases about Reg. FD was "[w]e believe that the practice of selective disclosure leads to a loss of investor confidence in the integrity of our capital markets." Hence, the introduction of Reg. FD.

Reg. FD Stipulations

The objective of Reg. FD is to ensure that all market participants—investors, analysts, and brokers—have access to material news *at the same time.* The scope and format of this book precludes printing the full text of Reg. FD in this chapter. A written copy of the regulation can be obtained from the SEC, or the text version can be retrieved from the agency's Web site: *www.sec.gov.*

Reg. FD prohibits your company from intentionally disclosing material, nonpublic information to specified types of securities markets professionals and stockholders unless the company publicly discloses this information simultaneously through fully accessible, nonexclusionary media. If your company unintentionally discloses material, nonpublic information to persons covered by Reg. FD, you must publicly disclose this information promptly. "Promptly" means as soon as possible. Once you are aware that such a disclosure has occurred, you must publicly disseminate it within 24 hours or before the opening of the next trading day, whichever is later. Public disclosure means the filing of a Form 8-K Report or dissemination of the information through another method (or a combination of methods) that is reasonably designed to provide broad, nonexclusionary distribution of the information to the public, which is generally thought to be a press release through one of the wire services.

In a speech given before the Compliance and Legal Division of the Securities Industry Association (SIA) soon after Reg. FD went into effect, the SEC's head of enforcement addressed the issue of the manner of transmitting material information:

> *Some people have suggested that FD is satisfied by the filing of a "procedural 8-K" announcing that all future FD disclosures* [sic] *will be posted to the company's Web site. I can tell you that the staff does not agree with this view.*

The SEC has stated, "[V]iolation of Reg. FD does not create a 'private right of action.'" That is, class-action plaintiffs cannot sue you for Reg. FD violations. If your company is suspected of engaging in "selective disclosure" in violation of Reg. FD, the agency can commence an enforcement proceeding against you (administratively or in federal court). In order to violate the regulation, your company must have acted recklessly or intentionally in making a selective disclosure. (Alternatively, there can be a violation by failure to make prompt disclosure of material information after inadvertently disclosing the information to securities professionals or investors.)

In practice, according to a speech to the SIA, the SEC's chief enforcer said:

> *An issuer's incorrect determination that information is not material must represent an "extreme departure" from standards of reasonable care in order for us to allege a violation.*

A Lesser-Known Stipulation

A lesser-known aspect of Reg. FD is the provision that allows selective disclosure "to any person who agrees to maintain the information in confidence." Thus, you don't necessarily have to stop sharing information on a selective basis. The party or parties to whom you have made this selective disclosure are bound by the regulation not to disclose or trade on the information until it has been made public under the terms of the regulation. Could this "vouchsafe" type of disclosure give the informed party an advantage over other investors, even if they cannot/do not disclose the information, and do not trade your company's stock? With respect to thinly traded stocks like yours, we think you have given the informed party an advantage. Don't make a "vouchsafe" disclosure to anyone. Ever.

It's About You

Think also about whose conduct Reg. FD is intended to regulate. Again, from the SEC's Enforcement Chief's talk to the SIA:

> *Regulation FD is not about the broker/dealer community. . . . Regulation FD speaks directly to issuers and their representatives, and requires that when they communicate material, non-public information to securities industry professionals or shareholders, they do so publicly, not selectively. Regulation FD places the responsibility for avoiding selective disclosure and the risks of engaging in it, SQUARELY ON THE ISSUER.*

Later in the speech, the chief enforcer talked about disclosure in the form of "indirect guidance" from a company:

> *Providing a wink or nod, or a coded response calculated to convey indirectly information that cannot be disclosed directly is no different—and no more or less legal—than telling an analyst point-blank, "our earnings will be down 10% this quarter."*

Don't let anyone in your company ever "get cute" in an interview or in a speech about the company's financial performance.

If your company has a practice of reviewing and commenting on drafts of reports prepared by an analyst or on an analyst's forecasting model, our advice is to discontinue doing so. That practice is too close to the line, and while it might not put you in FD jeopardy, it can cause you time and money responding to an SEC query about such a practice. We recommend prohibiting this activity (see below).

Who Is Subject to Reg. FD?

Besides informal blandishments ("keep your mouth shut" and "don't get cute"), your company needs a published set of practices and procedures governing disclosure. You must dictate who are *recipients* of material information triggering the public disclosure obligation. (Public disclosure requirements can also be triggered under the general antifraud rules because of a leak of information.) Those subject to Reg. FD are

- Anyone employed by or associated with a broker/dealer.
- Anyone employed by or associated with investment managers, investment advisors and consultants, and investment companies, trustees, and fiduciaries of investment funds shareholders.

You must state those parties who are not subject to Reg. FD. They are

1. Persons who do have a contractual or professional duty to keep confidence, such as attorneys, accountants, and bankers.
2. Those who expressly agree to maintain the confidentiality of information selectively disclosed to them.
3. Rating agencies, under certain conditions.
4. Members of the press and media.

Publish throughout your company the employees who are subject to the provisions of Reg. FD:

1. Directors, executives, and managers.

2. People performing investor relations or public relations functions.

3. Employees and/or agents who regularly communicate with shareholders or investment professionals.

Special Circumstances

The SEC recognizes that the dynamics of business activity create incidents and relationships that are fluid and of short duration. A regulation that has some indistinct aspects will create concerns about how or when it applies in the ebbing and flowing of transactions and communication. What follows is our take on three areas of concern about Reg. FD.

OTHER EMPLOYEES.   Statements made by other employees are not subject to Reg. FD unless made when they are acting at the direction of one of your executives or managers. But what about statements nonsubject employees (salespersons, buyers, human resources staffers) make to customers, suppliers, prospective employees, and others? We assume that your employees have been indoctrinated never to reveal any information about your company that could put it at a competitive disadvantage. Those specific restraints ought to suffice with respect to Reg. FD compliance. Note that general antifraud rules cover insider trading. Disclosures of information by any employees can result in illegal tipping or the need to disclose the leaked information.

PRIVATE PLACEMENT DOCUMENTS.   In our view, those whom you retain to get private money and the investors they solicit are not FD-exempt recipients of material information. These parties will want to know more than you probably want to disclose anyway. Whether or not any information is nonpublic or public is the least of an angel's concern. Disclose the attendant placement documents to the SEC in a Form 8-K or by news release, since eventually the information will have to be disclosed in a registration statement anyway. This rule does not apply to private companies doing a private placement with an angel investor. Note that Reg. FD only applies to companies with securities registered under Section 12 of the Securities Exchange Act of 1934—basically, public companies. Disclosures in private placements by public companies are subject to Reg. FD. Reg. FD would not apply to the disclosure by a private company to angel investors.

THE MEDIA. Obviously, Reg. FD cannot prohibit disclosure to the media. The spirit of the regulation encourages disclosure to large segments of the media. We concur in all respects. It is unwise to think you have complied with Reg. FD provisions when you disclose material, nonspecific information to just a few reporters. How can you be assured that any of them will report on what you disclosed? More importantly, how do you know a report will be complete in context—or wholly accurate? One or just a few media baskets are not enough in which to place your material, nonpublic eggs. "Broadcast" your disclosures in the true meaning of that verb. Don't play favorites with the media. Let them get their scoops somewhere else.

Practices and Procedures

Your company needs a Reg. FD compliance manual. Here are recommendations on some of the things to address when prescribing practices and procedures that will ensure compliance.

- **Limit the number of designated spokespersons.** This is an effective means of eliminating selective disclosure.
- **Educate and train the spokespersons.** We recommend that your CFO and a member of the board's audit committee oversee this education and training. Your outside counsel should interview your trainees when they have completed

the training to determine whether they understand the provisions of Reg. FD and your company's compliance policy.

- **Use prepared material.** It is highly recommended that presentations be scripted; and include a list of items already known to the public as well as subjects that are appropriate for discussion because they are considered to be the details of prior disclosures. There should be a reminder list of items not to disclose.

- **Watch your stock.** During and after live meetings or teleconferences with investors and analysts, someone should be assigned to monitor the activity of your company's stock. A sudden change in the price could mean that something material and nonpublic was inadvertently disclosed.

- **Make news releases detailed.** In a news release about a matter, include as much detail as your business strategy permits so that you can discuss the matters with analysts, investors, and other persons subject to Reg. FD.

- **Use nondisclosure agreements.** When you intend to cover confidential information with an outside party, have them sign a nondisclosure agreement.

- **Don't comment on the validity of an analyst's models.** This raises the same concerns as selective disclosure. If there are *factual* mistakes about a nonmaterial or publicly disclosed matter, you can correct them.

- **Remember the duty to update.** There is no change in the company's duty to update under Reg. FD. If a previous statement is no longer accurate but persons continue to rely on the statement, your company should consider updating the public on this change.

Penalties for Violations

The statutory section (Section 32) of the Securities Exchange Act of 1934 for criminal penalties regarding violations of that law or any rule or regulation thereunder provides for fines of not more than $1,000,000 or imprisonment not more than 10 years or both, except that when the violator is not a natural person, the fine may be up to $2,500,000.

According to Section 21(d) of the Securities Exchange Act, a third-tier violation results in a civil penalty not exceeding $100,000 for a natural person or $500,000 for any other person or the gross amount of pecuniary gain to the defendant. This section deals with a Commission action against a person who appears to have violated any rule or regulation under the 1934 Act.

The Real Challenge of Reg. FD

Sell side research was being held in low regard by experienced investors before Reg. FD was introduced. We discussed our concerns about broker/dealer analysts in Chapter 4. Portfolio managers who are interested in your company conduct their own research about it. They will collect data and information from sources other than broker/dealer research departments. They might talk to your customers, suppliers, creditors, and competition. None of them are constrained by the provisions of Reg. FD when they are asked about your company.

The real challenge of complying with Reg. FD is in responding to informed questions from enterprising buy side researchers, questions based on what they have already discerned from other sources. When you are asked a question based on some data or information acquired from outside your company, it will most likely be couched as an inference:

Since you have purchased 100 more boxcars of adaptable widgets than you bought last year at this time, can I infer that you are ramping up production?

Some companies might respond to the manner in which the inference was reached:

Some people might think so, if they thought an increase in such inventory was evidence enough to make such inference.

This is not being cute. Too clever? Maybe; but they haven't kissed off a potential investor with some form of "no comment." You need to take your counsel's advice about responding to questions from the diligent "pick-and-shovel" investor. In all likelihood, their advice will be to respond in this manner:

> *Our answer to that could be considered a material disclosure.*
> *We have no comment at this time.*

Analysts who, prior to Reg. FD, relied on extensive guidance from a target company now have to spend time and effort doing their own fundamental research. The burden of FD compliance rests squarely on your shoulders, but the burden of estimating earnings has been shifted from your back to the analyst's back. Where it should have always been. Now there is movement toward a wider range of earnings estimates. We can hope that this movement will reduce, if not eliminate, consensus risk.

Here is another fact of public company life under Reg. FD: You must have a firm policy about the manner in which you answer informed, inferential questions about your company.

Remember that Reg. FD is intended to regulate your behavior. There are very few sanctions for analysts or investors who misuse company information. Except in the context of violating the rules about insider trading.

INSIDER TRADING

Many people have the right to possess inside information, that is, information that is material and nonpublic. Most are not permitted to use the inside information for an investment advantage until that information is publicly disclosed. If they do otherwise, they are likely to have violated insider-trading regulations. Reg. FD augments, not replaces, SEC regulations prohibiting insider trading. The SEC instituted Reg. FD because in its opinion selective disclosure was essentially the "legal twin" of insider trading. The SEC's position is that it will not permit investors to profit from material, nonpublic information, as opposed to skill, acumen, and diligence. The distinction between a violation of Reg. FD and a violation of insider trading provisions is whether someone *acts* on the nonpublic (confidential) disclosure. The prohibition against insider trading is a major aspect of the Securities Exchange Act of 1934. With respect to insider trading violations, the SEC carries a big stick and does not walk softly.

Who Is an Insider?

An insider, according the Securities Exchange Act of 1934, is an officer or director of a public company. An insider is also any person or entity owning 10 percent or more of any class of a company's shares. The trading of a company's stock by an insider is regulated by the SEC. At the time you qualify as an insider, the SEC requires you to file *Form 3*. *Form 4* must be filed each time you buy or sell the company stock, and at the end of every year a *Form 5* must be filed by any person (or entity) that qualified as an insider anytime during that year.

In enforcement terms, the SEC also considers as an insider anyone who possesses material, nonpublic information. Also, anyone who trades stock based on material nonpublic information obtained from an insider is likely in violation of insider trading regulations. If an analyst breaches an agreement to keep information confidential by telling it to a client who trades on it, the analyst and the client have violated insider regulations. The analyst is guilty of illegal "tipping"; the client is guilty of insider trading.

The SEC employs very sophisticated surveillance systems to ensure compliance with its insider trading dictates. These systems track transactions across all markets in real time.

There is a system that stores data from sources all over the world. It is known as the Automatic Search and Match System (ASAM). ASAM's capabilities are remarkable and must never be underestimated. ASAM has commonly linked two or more seemingly unconnected people and uncovered an insider trading violation. If an official of your company intentionally, or recklessly, makes a selective disclosure to someone who rewards that official from subsequent profits made from the disclosure, you likely will have roadkill on the premises.

Rules 10b-5-1 and 10b-5-2

At the same time the SEC instituted Reg. FD, it also introduced two new rules: *10b-5-1* and *10b-5-2*. These new rules are intended to clarify when persons have violated insider-trading prohibitions.

Yes, it is illegal for someone who works for or advises your company to trade its stock based on material, nonpublic information. Some courts, however, did have questions about whether or not the SEC had to prove that your insider actually *acted on this knowledge,* or just knew about it when they traded in your company's stock. Rule10b-5-1 removes any questions. Now if somebody has material, nonpublic information about a stock and trades it, the SEC does not have to prove that the trader/investor acted on the basis of the information. It only needs to prove that the accused was aware of material, nonpublic information at the time of a transaction in your company's stock.

Rule 10b-5-2 reinforces the concept of "misappropriation of knowledge." This rule expressly forbids people who learn about material, nonpublic information on the basis of their relationship with your company from acting on it. This includes family members and other nonbusiness relationships, as well as attorneys, accountants, employees, and consultants. The tangential issue of privileged communication between spouses is an area in which the SEC is not afraid to venture.

My Wife, the Tipster

One of the attorneys we interviewed for this book shared his favorite insider case with us.

The CEO of a mid-cap company explained to his wife why he was so busy and so preoccupied. He was dealing with a tender offer for his company. His wife remarked about the tender offer to her brother. The brother, who lived in a trailer park, related the news to several people in the trailer park. The brother and several of his neighbors bought the stock. They subsequently made substantial trading profits from the stock, which they promptly spent. The SEC discovered all the facts and proved in court that there had been an infraction of insider trading regulations. The court ordered penalties equal to three times the gains from the trades made by the wife's brother and neighbors.

Guess who was judgment-proof. Guess who had to cough up, even though she didn't act on the information. Guess who's not coming to dinner.

Investor relations consultant Howard Kalt, of Kalt, Rosen and Associates in San Francisco, reminds his clients that "[n]o trade is too small, nor is any fish, not to be caught in the SEC's surveillance nets." Work closely with your counsel and with your financial team to craft fail-safe insider trading practices and procedures.

SAFE HARBOR PROVISIONS

The laws governing fair disclosure and trading make public companies reluctant to share information with investors. This reluctance has been increased by the willingness of shareholders to sue emerging companies for allegedly making misleading public statements about future prospects.

In the early 1990s, there was an epidemic of class action and individually filed lawsuits brought against emerging companies by shareholders. These suits would charge that management had made misleading statements so as to intentionally or recklessly raise investors' expectations. Many of these suits were without merit, and several were likely filed at the instigation of those who could make money from litigation.

Legislators and regulators became aware that a lot of the lawsuits were brought by people who refused to face the consequences of their own bad judgment. Moreover, the costs of defending the suits were financially crippling to these emerging companies. In 1995, the Private Securities Litigation Reform Act was instituted to dissuade every Tom, Dick, and Mary who lost some money in the market from suing. The provisions of the Act generally have protected, to some extent, companies from undeserved lawsuits while still permitting suits buttressed by arguments of merit.

The 1995 Act provides a "safe harbor" for your company's making public projections or statements about the future. A practice that has evolved from the Act is the declaring of a disclaimer when announcing or discussing news that may be considered a forward-looking statement. This extra piece of dialogue is referred to as the Safe Harbor statement.

Some suggested wordings for Safe Harbor statements are provided in Appendix 8–A. Many companies have chosen to err on the side of the extraneous with respect to including Safe Harbor statements in almost all their briefings and press releases. There are some issues with respect to Safe Harbor statements that should be considered.

Avoid Blanket Statements

A boilerplate statement intended as blanket cover for an accompanying Webcast, press release, or conference is not an inoculation. Experienced investors and the courts expect companies to be conscientious about their disclosure practices. Be precise when informing your audiences about the nature of your disclosure. In each forward-looking statement, point out the specific items that are characterized by opportunity, risk, or financial changes. The safe harbor is based in part upon accompanying the forward-looking statement with meaningful cautionary statements identifying important factors that could cause actual results to differ materially from those in the forward-looking statement or, in the case of oral forward-looking statements, referring to a written document containing such cautionary statements.

Don't Refer to Separate Documents

We have observed instances when a company spokesperson has referred to a separate document when making a forward-looking statement: "We expect to extend our coverage to four other countries, subject to the risks disclosed in our most recent 10-K." This kind of reference does not provide the speaker with Safe Harbor protection. The risks must be disclosed at the time you are imparting information and spelled out in the press release about the topic. For written statements, the Safe Harbor provisions and cautionary statements must accompany the written disclosure. In the case of an oral forward-looking statement, the cautionary statements can be included with the oral statement or there can be a reference to written material containing appropriate cautionary statements. You cannot refer to separate documents when the forward-looking statement is written.

Avoid Qualifying Words

Take care to eliminate those words that make a disclosure seem so conditional that it is meaningless with respect to valuing your company's prospects. Avoid "maybe," "perhaps," "possibly," "if," "conceivably," "feasibly," and "imaginably."

DON'T FALL SILENT

Earlier in this book, we advised (somewhat rudely) that sometimes you should keep your mouth shut. We think that is good advice but not when there is a change in your operations that can be considered material. Not disclosing that change could violate the letter and the spirit of disclosure regulations. Remaining silent about something that can adversely affect the company may provide grounds for shareholder suits. Forms 10-K, 10-Q, and 8-K provide one means of disclosing a significant change; in fact, Forms 10-K and 10-Q have parts that can require the disclosure of anticipated, material changes. Again, when making a cautionary statement, be precise.

Because of the ability to refer to written documents when making oral forward-looking statements and because there may be written statements that are forward-looking, the SEC reports of many companies now contain cautionary statements under a "Risk Factors" section.

In Chapter 7 (page 87) we cited *The ValueReporting Revolution*. In this book, the authors address and refute the 10 most common reasons executives give for limiting disclosure:[1]

Reason/Excuse 1: The Market Cares Only about Earnings

In our survey of U.S. analysts and investors, "earnings" tops the list of the most important performance measures. But closely on its heels are five other financial measures that analysts and investors rank very high as well: R&D investments, cash flow, costs, capital expenditures, and segment performance. Four nonfinancial measures also rank high: market growth, new product development, market share, and statements of strategic goals.

The results from the other 13 countries in that survey, as well as the results from the banking, insurance, and high-tech industry surveys, showed similar, if not identical, rankings. For example, seven of the Top Ten Hit Parade of measures in the high-tech survey are nonfinancial. . . . The market clearly cares about a wide range of performance measures and wishes it could get better information on most of them.

Reason/Excuse 2: We Already Report a Lot of Information

It's not a question of how much information is being reported. It's whether the *right* information is being reported. Recognizing that companies must abide by varying reporting requirements depending on their country of origin, and that some of this information may be of marginal use to investors, they often report a significant amount of information that really isn't all that useful to the market. The solution is painfully obvious. Replace that information with other information that investors *will* find useful.

Corporate executives in the United States can legitimately claim that they face more regulatory reporting requirements than their European and Asian counterparts. But as the banking and insurance industry surveys showed, the Information Gaps in both the United States and Europe are virtually the same. U.S. bank and insurance company executives fare no better in meeting the market's information needs along such measures as customer retention, customer penetration, risk management practices, market risk exposure (especially interesting in light of FAS 133), performance by business segment, and economic profit. This is not all that surprising because accounting regulations don't even cover most of these measures. It does clearly demonstrate, however, the difference between the quantity and the relevance of the information provided.

Reason/Excuse 3: Once We Start Reporting Something, We Can't Stop

If the market finds a certain piece of performance information useful, it will certainly want more of the same. As Swiss Re's Walter Kielholz notes in Chapter 1, "Once it's out there, you can't get rid of it." Wouter de Vries, head of investor relations at Royal Dutch Shell, agrees: "There's no going back."

Management serves its own best interests when it responds to the market's desire for more information because progress on that measure will have a positive effect on the company's stock price. If, however, a particular measure becomes irrelevant, or a better one comes along, the company has no reason to continue to report on it. Management will, of course, have to explain why the company has stopped. Decisions to no longer report on a performance measure should be made very carefully as the value of information grows when it is in the context of a historical trend line and comparable to competitors.

Reason/Excuse 4: Producing and Reporting Information Cost a Lot

Thanks to the Internet, the cost of providing information to the market will continue to decrease dramatically. Generalizing from Moore's Law, the cost of providing information over the Internet goes down by about half every 18 months. Shell sees this as an opportunity to significantly reshape communications in the future. Investor relations head Wouter de Vries foresees "reporting as being increasingly tailored for every stakeholder and investor" with customized information based on the user's profile.

The real issue here is the cost of generating the information, not reporting it. Certain measures, such as customer retention or process quality, are often difficult to measure and require the development of new measurement methodologies, which can cost a lot indeed. Managers must then decide whether having this information for internal decision-making purposes justifies the cost of generating it. If managers find that it does, making the information available to the market adds very little incremental cost.

Reason/Excuse 5: No Matter How Much We Report, the Market Always Wants More

This is simply not true. The size of the Information Gap— the difference between the importance the market places on a measure and how satisfied it is with the information it gets— varies enormously. Most of the analysts and investors in our global survey said they were generally satisfied with the information they receive on the important measures of earnings and capital expenditures, as well as on the relatively unimportant measure of environmental compliance. There were a few exceptions, but mostly in countries with less strict reporting requirements.

Similar levels of satisfaction were found in the banking and insurance surveys where the Information Gap was virtually nonexistent for earnings, loan loss ratio (banks), claims ratio (insurance companies), assets under management, investment performance, core deposit growth (banks), regulatory reputation, and plans for growth. Note that not all of these measures are required by regulation and that some are rather qualitative. Satisfying the market's information needs clearly doesn't require regulations and precise numbers. In the high-tech survey, analysts reported satisfaction with the information they get on 19 of the 37 measures, and investors were satisfied on 11. Most of these measures, however, were not considered very important.

Reason/Excuse 6: Bad Numbers Will Hurt Our Stock Price

This is true. If the market believes that a financial or non-financial measure is important to value creation, bad numbers will hurt the company's stock price, even if earnings remain strong. However, improved performance on the measure can have a positive effect on a company's stock price, even when earnings remain weak. There is no escaping the fact: Markets reward and punish companies based on performance, whether it's earnings or any of the other important measures. That's what markets are all about.

Reason/Excuse 7: Some of These Measures Aren't Very Reliable

It's true that reporting no information is better than reporting bad information. It's also true that most companies don't have adequate internal measurement systems for some key performance dimensions, particularly the nonfinancial ones. Chapter 7 described this type of Quality Gap for the high-tech industry in detail.

With sufficient effort, however, a company can nearly always identify and track measures that have sufficient reliability. Just look at the success certain companies have had in implementing balanced scorecard systems for internal use: AT&T, Bank of America, Boots the Chemist, Ciba Geigy, Ericsson, General Motors, Johnson & Johnson, Kmart, Lufthansa, Novo Nordisk, Roche, SBC Warburg, Swiss Telecom, and United Technologies.

Reason/Excuse 8: Our Competitors Will Use This Information to Our Disadvantage

It's a possibility, but a highly exaggerated one. If a company wants information on a competitor, it has many legitimate avenues for getting it, including the Internet, a consulting firm, or hiring an executive away from a competitor.

A study done for the Australian building products company Pioneer found that at least one company in that industry reported on virtually every single performance measure. As people sometimes say, "It's a secret to everybody or it's a secret to nobody." Even if reporting to the market gave competitors information they didn't already have or couldn't get, actually using the information for competitive advantage is much easier said than done. Changing strategies and behaviors is no mean feat.

Reason/Excuse 9: Our Customers and Suppliers Could Learn How Much Money We're Making

So what? They probably have a pretty good idea already. Suppliers and customers care far less about how much money a company makes than about the economic advantages of doing business with that company. If they perceive a real benefit from the relationship, they'll stay in it. If more attractive choices come along, they'll pursue them, regardless of how much or little money the company in question makes. Customers and suppliers respond to competition in the product markets, not information in the capital markets.

Reason/Excuse 10: We'll Get Sued

In the United States especially, the risk of litigation poses a very legitimate concern. Tort lawyers have had a field day blackmailing companies who release forward-looking information, even when they do so with all the proper disclaimers. The Safe Harbor provision of litigation reform legislation passed in 1995 aimed at reducing this risk. How much positive effect it will have remains to be seen.

Experience to date suggests that a real and lasting solution remains elusive. For every day the market was open in 1998, a company was named as a defendant in a lawsuit. As one might expect, high-technology companies get sued the most frequently. Among all companies, almost 60 percent of all such suits allege accounting misdeeds and more than half allege insider sales. [Endnote omitted.]

Commenting on such a high rate of litigation in the post–Safe Harbor legislation years, Joseph A. Grundfest, a former SEC commissioner, said, "People frequently ask why the Private Securities Litigation Reform Act of 1995 has not reduced the volume of litigation. . . . Plaintiffs claim that fraud is common in today's stock market and point to many examples of accounting restatements and trading by corporate insiders. . . . Defendants claim that honest conduct in volatile markets is often mistaken for fraud, and some courts have failed to implement the Reform Act properly because they don't subject plaintiff's complaints to sufficiently searching scrutiny." [Endnote omitted.]

Accounting fraud and insider trading may appear a bit removed from the call for greater transparency, but the litigious environment in the United States discourages some companies from providing more information to the market. Concerns about legal liabilities under state laws and uncertainty about how the federal court will interpret the Safe Harbor provision have kept managers from taking much comfort in this legislation. As a result, many legitimate concerns still exist about providing more information, particularly forward-looking statements. It's clearly an area that regulators should examine more closely.

THE PROXY PROCESS

A *proxy form* is a document that permits your shareholders to confer upon another person their respective rights to vote their stock on corporate matters and shareholder proposals at shareholder meetings. The proxy form must be accompanied by a *proxy statement*. This form is an explanation of the material information that will be voted upon. It must be filed with the SEC for examination prior to its distribution to stockholders. The SEC does not require the filing in advance of proxy materials dealing only with the election of directors without opposition, the selection of accountants, any shareholder proposals included in accordance with SEC rules, and the approval of any stock plan for employees. The SEC will be reviewing the proxy statement to see that it includes all the material facts about the matter to be voted upon. SEC Regulation 14A governs the manner in which proxies must be solicited.

The SEC rules permit any holder of your voting stock or any group holding your voting stock to make an independent proxy solicitation without your or the board's permission or concurrence.

Types of Shareholders

Your company is required to distribute proxy forms and statements to every holder of your company's voting stock. Your shareholders of voting stock are not likely to be found in one convenient list. The three most common lists on which voting shareholders could be found are Registered Shareholders Lists, Objecting Beneficial Owners Lists (OBOL), and the Non-Objecting Beneficial Owners Lists (NOBOL).

> **Registered shareholders** are those shareholders that own shares in their own names and most likely have physical possession of their shares. The transfer agent will have an up-to-date listing of these shareholders.

> **OBOL** listees have their stock held for them by a custodian designated by their brokerage firm. This manner in which stocks are held is generally referred to as being held *in street name*. At the request of their stockbroker, these holders have signed a form requesting that their names not be disclosed to your company. Clients may sign an OBOL form as a means to retain privacy; however, they are just as likely to have signed

the form because their brokers asked them to do so. Why? Brokerage firms don't want to disclose the names of their clients as a matter of competitive practice. There are instances when a brokerage firm is retained by your company to offer rights distribution (such as a warrant). That brokerage company then has access to your shareholder list. It can put those names on its prospect lists. The OBOL arrangement prevents this because it permits your offer to be channeled only through an intermediary. The authorized intermediary for most public companies is:

Investor Communication Services
ADP Broker Services Group
51 Mercedes Way
Edgewood, NY 11717
(631) 254-7400

NOBOL listees are likely to be the largest number of registered holders of your voting stock. Their shares are held in street name, but they have not signed an OBOL form. Your NOBOL list also can be obtained from ADP Broker Services Group.

In this chapter we have advised you about how to be pro-active when complying with all of those disclosure requirements. The next chapter addresses the reactive strategies needed to combat the insidious Chat Room Pox.

NOTE

1. Robert G. Eccles, Robert H. Herz, E. Mary Keegan, and David M.H. Phillips, *The ValueReporting Revolution* (New York: John Wiley & Sons, 2001), pp. 203–208.

Selected Samples of Safe Harbor Statements

SAMPLE OF SAFE HARBOR STATEMENT (ALTERNATIVE 1)

Safe Harbor Statement Under the Private Securities Litigation Reform Act of 1995. This is an all-inclusive form suitable for any business:

> In accordance with the Safe Harbor provisions of the Private Securities Litigation Reform Act of 1995, the company notes that statements in this news release, and elsewhere, that look forward in time, which include everything other than historical information, involve risks and uncertainties that may affect the company's actual results of operations. The following important factors, among others that are discussed in company filings with the Securities and Exchange Commission, could cause actual results to differ materially from those set forth in the forward-looking statements:
>
> a) Intense competition may cause us to lose projects or result in decreased revenues;

b) We may not be able to hire qualified technical personnel;

c) The highly competitive market for technical personnel may increase our costs;

d) Our operating results may fluctuate significantly; and,

e) Acquisitions involve numerous risks, including the following:

(i) Difficulties in integration of the operations, technologies and products of the acquired companies;

(ii) The risk of diverting management's attention from normal daily operations of the business;

(iii) Risks of entering markets in which the company has no or limited direct prior experience and where competitors in such markets have stronger market positions; and

(iv) The potential loss of key employees of acquired companies.

SAMPLE OF SAFE HARBOR STATEMENT (ALTERNATIVE 2)

This statement is only good for oral statements:

This presentation contains forward-looking statements within the meaning of Section 21A of the Securities Act of 1933, as amended, and Section 21E of the Securities Exchange Act of 1934, as amended, and are subject to the safe harbors created thereby. Such statements involve certain risks and uncertainties associated with an emerging company. Actual results could differ materially from those projected in the forward-looking statements as a result of risk factors discussed in the company's reports that will be on file with the US Securities and Exchange Commission (including but not limited to the report on Form 10-K).

SAMPLE OF SAFE HARBOR STATEMENT (ALTERNATIVE 3)

This form is suitable for companies who do business in countries other than the United States:

> This news release contains forward-looking statements within the meaning of Section 21A of the Securities Act of 1933, as amended, and section 21E of the Securities Exchange Act of 1934, as amended. Such statements are subject to risks and uncertainties that could cause actual results to vary materially from those projected in the forward-looking statements. The company may experience significant fluctuations in future operating results due to a number of economic, competitive, and other factors, including, among other things, the size and timing of customer orders, changes in laws, new or increased competition, delays in new products, production problems, changes in market demand, market acceptance of new products, seasonal product purchases, and changes in foreign exchange rates. These factors, and other factors, which could materially affect the company and its operations, are included in the company's filings with the Securities and Exchange Commission and are incorporated herein.

CHAPTER 9

The Chat Room Pox

I N CHAPTER 6, WE ADVISE TO BE CONSTANTLY VIGILANT about "pump-and-dump" schemes. The Internet permits these schemes to be implemented easily among unscrupulous brokers and professional criminals using chat rooms and message boards.

BLOWING SMOKE

Just as insidious are the dialogues conducted in the chat rooms and message boards where the goal may or may not be pump and dump. Over half of the "inside insights" flowing through the chat rooms or being posted are by persons whose identities are obscured by anonymity (as well as by the smoke they are blowing). These "sources" might not be career criminals or capital markets miscreants; however, whether they are just passing time or up to some chicanery, they can impact the market for your company's stock.

Your Primary Concern

In *NEXT: The Future Just Happened*,[1] author Michael Lewis details the background of the SEC's case against Cedar Grove, New Jersey, teenager Jonathan Lebed for stock market fraud. Lebed bought stocks with an E*Trade account, and then posted messages on Yahoo Finance, using fictitious names, recommending the stocks. Lebed made about $800,000 from late 1999 through February 2000. The average volume of the small companies in which he traded was about 60,000 shares a day. On the days he posted his messages, some issues traded more than a million shares. After the chaos created by this aberrant market behavior, the shares of the subject companies receded below the prices at which they were trading when Lebed began posting. It seemed there was nothing that the target companies could do, once the frenzied trading began.

The SEC eventually settled with Lebed. They required him to give up only $285,000. The case begged the question whether rumors posted on the Internet constitute financial fraud but do not if they are passed on in the barbershop or on CNBC. Yes, but Lebed used fictitious names when he posted his messages. So? A lot of people use fictitious names on the Internet.

Whether or not this chat room and posting activity is illegal should not be your primary concern. Your concern is its impact on how your company's stock is valued and traded. Your concern might be expressed with the perplexed query:

> *Why would anyone buy or sell a stock solely on just what they saw posted or discussed on the Internet?*

Because they're human; therefore, they're lazy, impressionable, bored, and greedy. Some people have made a very good living playing to people's propensity to "invest, then investigate." The Internet has enhanced the capability of those people inclined to take advantage of that propensity. These people have no regard for damage done to investors or stock values.

Fanning Flames of Grievance

The Internet insurgents may not always have the objective of affecting the value of your company's stock. There have been hundreds of cases of malicious intent from former employees and the disgruntled still on the payroll. Another aggravating group might be composed of dissatisfied customers who have slipped through your customer-relations activities or your product warranty programs. You even may be, heaven help you, the target of some activist group.

Dealing with these types of hostiles will generally not involve the SEC. But even when the SEC does get involved, your opinion about how they view their role with respect to your concerns may not be correct.

Who Does the SEC Protect?

We emphasize: *cyberspace scams, schemes, and rumors usually involve microcap stocks.* The SEC continues to be more adept at early identification of and intervention in Internet fraud. Keep in mind, however, that the SEC's role is to protect investors from fraudulent activity, *not your company.* There are instances when investors who were victims of investment frauds have had some of their losses returned. There have been no instances when the courts or any agency has mandated the restoration of the market value of a stock diminished by fraudulent activity or the madness of crowds.

WHAT YOUR COMPANY SHOULD DO AND NOT DO

There have been so many Internet attempts to manipulate stock prices that an accepted set of practices has evolved to counter the scammers and neutralize the smoke blowers. These practices are grounded in practicality and in law. No one has the time to track down the identity of every purveyor of misinformation, nor can any company afford the legal costs of challenging every rumor or opinion as slander or libel.

Meet this problem with the same reasoned judgment you use when you confront the other challenges to your company's growth.

Wrong News Can Never Be Good

Don't let anyone in your company think that misinformation from the Web can sometimes benefit your company. There is no such thing as a false rumor that will bring an enduring increase in the price of your stock. Once a price-enhancing rumor is dispelled about a stock, the stock's price always retreats to a level below what it was before the rumor was circulated. This is always the case.

The Appropriate Response

Don't ever go on a message board or into a chat room to refute what was said on those sites about your company—not ever. You aren't equipped to fight guerilla insurgents, who have little to lose, in their jungle. Your every word will sink you further into a morass, from which there may be no escape.

Respond through appropriate channels and with reasoned arguments. The appropriate channels are press releases, press conferences, e-mail, letters, teleconferences, and your own Web site. Take advantage of that Web site, and use the financial reporting section to refute the smoke and garbage. If these items might have a severe impact on your company's well being, counter them in a banner format at the top of your site.

Address these matters at length with supporting documentation in the next Form 10-Q you file. If the matter could or is having a severe impact on your business or stock price, file a Form 8-K as soon as possible.

You may be in violation of a filing requirement if you do not get an 8-K out.

Don't waste time and money preparing responses to generalities or to petty, snide remarks that might not even be about you.

Address the items that impinge on the reputation of your company or impact the price of its stock.

Appropriate Action

In addition to quickly filing a Form 8-K, notify

1. Your local district attorney.
2. Your attorney.
3. The nearest SEC office.
4. The exchanges where your stock trades.
5. Your market makers.
6. Your state office of securities regulation.
7. The accounting firm who does your audits.

Be prepared to immediately provide these parties with all relevant documentation about the content, the site(s), and the date and time you became aware of the misinformation. Tell them what you have done and are doing.

Remember, even if the perpetrators of an Internet deception are caught and convicted, there is still the likelihood of lingering residual harm to your company. You and your management team must have in place practices and procedures that will quickly identify as well as prevent such occurrences.

Web Surveillance

One practice is to retain a Web surveillance company, whose services are just like those of a clipping service. The Web surveillance firms monitor the Internet for mention of your company and provide you with the full text of that information and the location(s) of such. The scope of these firms' surveillance is one factor in retaining one, but just as important is how quickly they provide you with those mentions of your company with the sites and sources.

Typical Charges

eWatch charges $3,600 per coverage. Coverage includes five available services:

1. **Web Pubs.** Coverage includes monitoring of thousands of editorial news sites on the Web. New Web sites will be added continuously.

2. **Newsgroups.** Coverage includes more than 66,000 Usenet groups and 15,000 Electronic Mailing Lists.

3. **Online Service Forums.** Coverage currently includes America Online and CompuServe.

4. **Investor Message Boards.** Coverage includes discussion about your organization on the investor message boards on Raging Bull, Yahoo!, Motleyfool, and Silicon Investor.

5. **WebWatch.** Automated daily monitoring of changes in customer-specified sites on the World Wide Web. Web publications, search engines, and E-zines do not apply.

ANNUAL PRICES

	10 Users	25 Users
Each Coverage	$3,600	$8,550
All 5 Coverages	$16,200	$38,475
Report Redistribution Rights	$2,500	$5,000

- User is the person with access to the eWatch report.
- For an agency a user profile is one of the agency's clients.
- Search criteria per each user or profile is unlimited.
- eWatch charges are all-inclusive and annual.
- There is a minimum of 10 users per subscription.
- Sample reports are available at *www.ewatch.com*; click on "Sample Report" on the left-hand side.
- One-month trials are available for $395 per service.

Restrictions on Employees

Controlling what is communicated from your company will help deter pump and dumpers, smoke blowers, and time wasters from obtaining information that they can play on with willful misinterpretation.

The most effective controlling measure is an e-mail policy that is unambiguous and easy to enforce. Your company should strictly control what is permitted for transmission on the net, and who is permitted to prepare and send Internet traffic from your company.

Richard Block and Meredith Steigman of the New York law firm Winthrop, Stimson, Putnam, & Roberts have written and spoken on the issue of e-mail and the workplace. In an article in the June 2000 issue of the *Journal of Investment Consulting,* they remind management that an e-mail policy should balance your need to manage the use of the computer system and protect the company against employee unlawful behavior, versus the need to have a work environment with good employee morale.

Block and Steigman remind companies that an effective e-mail policy should do the following:[2]

Explain that the computer system is company property and may be used only for business purposes.

Let employees know that e-mail will be monitored without further notice to employees to ensure that the computer system is being used for business purposes only.

- Stipulate that employees have no right to privacy in any communication sent or received over the company e-mail system.
- Dispel the erroneous beliefs that e-mail is ephemeral and there are means to conceal e-mail messages.
- Dispel the assumptions about the confidentiality of passwords, and explain your company's right to use its own passwords to monitor the system.
- Detail what kind of language should not be contained in any e-mail message.

- Inform your employees about the prohibition against using e-mail to solicit or campaign for agendas or programs not approved by your company.

- Explain that only company-authorized personnel are entitled to access all e-mail messages.

- Warn employees that they may be disciplined for unauthorized use of the Internet or the e-mail system.

- Stress the importance of not disclosing proprietary information over the e-mail system or the Internet.

Maryann Waryjas, an attorney with Jenner and Block in Chicago, suggested a similar policy to members of the National Investor Relations Institute (NIRI). Waryjas reminded NIRI that because postings placed on the Internet display a company's return address, any e-mail transmitted by a company must reflect and adhere to all of that company's standards and policies.

Your policy must be made known to all of your employees. Put a waiver statement on your system, and also require that all employees stipulate with signature that they have read the policy and agree to comply with all of its provisions.

ONE MORE TIME

Emerging companies like yours are the most susceptible to cyberspace scams, schemes, and rumors that could do lasting harm. Constant vigilance is the most effective countering strategy. Sound internal policies and rapid responses are your most effective preventive and countering tactics.

NOTES

1. Michael Lewis, *NEXT: The Future Just Happened* (New York: W. W. Norton, 2001).

2. Richard Block and Meredith Steigman, "Computers, E-Mail and the Workplace: Treacherous Legal Territory for Investment Consultants?," *Journal of Investment Consulting* 2 (2, June 2000): 1.

Corporate Practices

CHAPTER 10

Establishing an Investor Relations Department

YOU NEED SOME KIND OF PROGRAM to inform investors and shareholders about how you are increasing shareholder value. At a minimum, your company needs an investor relations program to assist in the preparation of the 10-K annual report, the 10-Q quarterly reports, and the public disclosure of material developments. These activities do not require establishing and staffing a distinct IR department. Many IR functions can be handled by your CFO, the securities counsel, and a contracted IR professional. Meeting your IR requirements in this manner should ensure compliance with reporting and disclosure requirements.

At some point in your growth, circumstances will dictate an in-house IR department. The major advantage for having an in-house IR department is controlling confidentiality. For this reason, we recommend that the head of the IR department report directly to the CEO.

THE IR DEPARTMENT'S ACTIVITIES

Your IR department should be assigned the following activities:

1. Assisting the finance department in overseeing filings with the SEC.

2. Assisting the outside auditing firm in formatting reports, and providing the liaison between your company's departments and the outside auditors.

3. Preparing and distributing the annual report and the Management Discussion and Analysis (MD&A).

4. Creating and disseminating all news releases about material developments.

5. Scheduling and organizing the annual meeting.

6. Scheduling and preparing all teleconferences, road shows, and investor presentations.

7. Preparing and distributing due diligence reports and media kits.

8. Working with the CFO and counsel to ensure an effective system for monitoring financial reporting and disclosure.

9. Working with other departments within the company to ensure that they are complying with all reporting and disclosure requirements.

Everyone on the Same Page, All the Time

Please reread suggested activity 9. We have argued, very effectively, over the years that "[a]ll other aspects of corporate communications are subelements of investor relations." That includes advertising, general announcements, new product introductions, and crisis management. We do not argue that these functions should ever report to an IR department. We do insist, however, that the directors dictate a policy requiring the IR department to be given adequate advance notice of any forthcoming communications. This includes advertising and sales campaigns. This policy is not ever intended to get IR's approval or sign-off. It is simply a best practices policy to ensure that IR gets an appropriate "heads-up" notification. This is another reason why we recommend that IR report directly to the CEO.

QUALIFICATIONS FOR HEAD OF AN IR DEPARTMENT

The overriding question about a candidate to direct your IR activities is

Does this person truly understand our business?

Would you hire that person for a sales, marketing, or product development position? If your answer is no, rethink why you were considering this person for the IR job. Keep in mind that an effective IR strategy requires an IR head who "walks the walk" and "talks the talk."

Another critical question is *will this person be a team player?* One of the IR head's functions will be blending the messages of disparate departments into a common, unified voice. That requires enlisting the assistance of other key players in your company. An aspect of your human relations concern is leadership ability. Can the candidate command respect and motivate a wide range of different personalities to act in the best interests of your company?

Background and Education

A bachelor's degree in business, law, or accounting is evidence that the candidate has a basic understanding of corporate business practices. This background is also helpful when dealing with high-net-worth individuals and institutional investors. A degree in journalism indicates writing skill and a knowledge of communications media.

No less than five years' experience in investor relations is necessary for someone upon whom you will depend to run your IR activities. That experience should include some management, as well as having successfully worked in all the activities associated with investor relations: writing, disclosure, compliance, and planning meetings and teleconferences. A candidate with extensive investor relations time with a single large corporation may have acquired expertise in just one activity. That person might not appreciate the interdependence and dynamics of an effective investor relations program, the appreciation of which is vital for an IR director in an emerging company. A candidate who manages the IR program for an emerging company will have to tolerate the mundane tasks associated with administration and with the preparation of reports and presentations.

Understanding the Securities Industry

An understanding of capital markets and corporate finance must be demonstrated. That knowledge is best acquired by working for a broker/dealer firm or with an investment management company. It can also be acquired by experience with an accounting or consulting firm. We recommend that you do not hire a "corporate communications professional" whose understanding of finance is limited. We have often had a client company CEO tell us, "I can teach them what they need to know." In almost every instance, what was meant was

> *They just need to know how to punctuate the written stuff. I will tell them what to say.*

This ventriloquist approach to IR staffing fails every time.

We do not advise on-the-job training about finance and markets, unless you have time to devise and oversee a structured training program. The circumstances are somewhat different with respect to compliance. Yes, the candidate does need a working knowledge of appropriate SEC law. Obtaining such is a challenge, but a candidate can grasp the concept of mandated rules much more easily than the subtleties and dynamics of investors and markets. You can "bring someone up to speed" on what to do and what not to do with respect to compliance.

Versatile and Adaptable

In addition to an ability to communicate effectively within all media and with various constituencies, you should ascertain the candidate's willingness to travel extensively. This willingness is often over-looked in the task of determining the other qualifications. There will be many times during the year when the IR head will be accompanying you and your senior executives on visits and pre-sentations to investors. There will be an equal amount of time during which your IR representative will be traveling alone.

Your IR department head should have a temperament that can accommodate criticism (constructive or otherwise.) After all, this is a person who will be reporting to you. We suggest that your associates and your significant other have the opportunity to inter-view qualified candidates. They probably will discern which can-didate will be the "best fit" with you.

Staffing the IR Department

The staff of an emerging company's IR department is similar to that of a microcap investment manager: slim or none. When starting a department, you should limit the staff to one other per-son whom you have ascertained will work well with the IR direc-tor. At a minimum, this person should demonstrate skill with word processing, spreadsheet calculations, and PowerPoint pres-entation graphics. The temperament, collegiality, and cooperative attitude required of the IR director are equally important for this person to have.

MEASURING THE EFFECTIVENESS OF YOUR IR PROGRAM

Like advertising and other promotional expenses, the return on investor relations is not easily measured. Seldom will you see your IR activities immediately reflected by an increase in the market price of your stock. Remember that the market is a forward-looking discounting system composed of much information and many opin-ions. We have learned that the manner in which it assigns values to different stocks is complicated. Good news about your com-pany may move within the market in nanoseconds or in weeks.

The best measure of the effectiveness of your IR efforts could be what the price of your stock is relative to what it was six months ago, or how it compares to the stock of a similar company.

You should, from time to time, compare the value of your company's equity to that of companies in your industrial peer group or sector. If your stock's price-to-earnings ratio is higher than a company that has a pattern of financial performance similar to yours, then you have achieved a return on your investment in IR activities. If your stock's P/E ratio is less than that of a similar performing peer company, you ought to review the program. We recommend comparing your share prices to those of sector or microcap peers. We see little value in comparing the movement of your share price to the movement of major market indices. The only fact that you might possibly discover is that yours is the hot ticket (or the dog) of the month. The hot stocks of the month seldom hold their price advantage. Of course, that market fickleness is good news if your stock was barking.

We insist that our clients institute a more extensive system and process for comparative measures of stock prices and performance. We work to construct a representative sample of peer or same-sector companies. Our clients then compile for each company the six-month figures in the following categories:

1. Growth rate of revenue.
2. Revenue per share.
3. P/E ratio.
4. Growth rate of earnings.
5. Earnings as a percentage of revenues.
6. Current ratio.
7. Debt-to-equity ratio.
8. Current-assets-to-current-liabilities ratio.
9. Cash flow per share.

Compare your company's measures with those of the sample group. Look then at the relationship between each company's numbers and their listed share prices. Compare these numbers and stock prices to those of your company. You should be able to determine if there are any apparent anomalies.

If this study reveals that your stock is undervalued relative to the sample group or to some of the companies in the group, make this known to your targeted brokers and institutional investors.

MONITORING THE EFFECTIVENESS OF YOUR IR ACTIVITIES

Another tracking system we recommend is easier to administer and provides ongoing evidence of investor interest. Maintain a system for tallying the things that logically correlate with interest in your company:

1. Number of investor inquiries.
2. Number of information packages requested.
3. Number of appointments made with the sell side.
4. Number of appointments made with the buy side.
5. Number of conference calls set up.
6. Number of conference call participants.
7. Number of presentations made.
8. Number of attendees at presentations.

TRACKING YOUR STOCK

The present market value of your stock may not be an accurate appraisal of the market's regard for your company's prospects, so measures other than price need to be monitored at least weekly. Those measures are

1. Changes in daily volume.
2. Changes in the number of shareholders.
3. Changes in shares held among institutions.

4. Changes in short positions.

5. Changes in the amount of odd-lot transactions.

6. A marked change in volatility.

7. Marked changes in price relative to the market.

8. Changes in the number of institutional owners.

The next two chapters prescribe and describe the critical activities of an effective investor relations program.

CHAPTER 11

Best Practices for News Releases

OTHER THAN THE SEC FORM 10-K, the news release is the most important form for disclosing *material* information. There are many occasions when the news release has greater importance than the SEC Form 10-Q. That is because many material-event news releases are issued in the interims between required 10-Q filing dates.

MATERIALITY, ONE MORE TIME

As defined in Chapter 8, information is deemed "material" when *there is a substantial likelihood that a reasonable shareholder would consider it important and that the information would have been viewed by the reasonable shareholder as having significantly altered the total mix of information made available.*

Circumstances and situations associated with what is required in your annual Management Discussion and Analysis (MD&A) are obviously material: changes in financial condition, capital expenditures, results in operations, known trends, events likely to come to fruition. The introduction of a new product, a new management structure, a merger, or a turn of fortune are some of the many instances that have to be considered material. A "turn of fortune" may not be the whim of a major customer or an act of nature. It could be a regulatory mandate. A change in accounting or financial reporting standards might very well be a turn of fortune.

Preparing a material-event news release requires disciplined, focused writing. Keep in mind the issue of materiality drives the content and focus of a news release. You should only report or describe a situation or circumstance within the confines of the material facts being disclosed. It is a best practice to avoid disclosing information about another separate material event in the same release.

Always Appear Savvy

It is also a best practice to avoid subjective appraisals or vague comments in the release. "The company expects next quarter's earnings to be more in line with management's expectations" is an egregious example. We didn't make that up. We have seen statements such as that too many times. This is not an example of what the SEC encourages as "forward-looking information." Be factual or be quiet.

Known, Likely, and Uncertain

The very best practice with respect to material news is not limiting releases to known events or situations. Disclosure duty within an MD&A requires addressing the likely and the uncertain. Make that same duty a part of your news release policy as well. This "no surprises" approach to disclosure enhances your appeal to experienced investors. Always report on a situation or circumstance that is presently known and is *reasonably likely to have a material effect on your business.* Again, focus on just that specific situation or circumstance, remembering that it is the subject of the news release and drives the content and focus.

Reasoned planning overrides IR just as it does any other business function. Reason dictates determining the effect or impact of likely events or uncertain ones. Keep your IR department in your contingency planning loop. They must be prepared to disclose quickly the effect or impact of an event such as a government over-throw in a country where you have extensive operations or that is a major supply source of raw materials.

Events of the fall of 2001 have heightened interest in how well companies plan for the unforeseen. Your board of directors may want to disclose parts of your overall contingency plan as it currently exists.

When There Is Good News

Always release good news as early in the week as possible. This leaves the investment community the rest of the week to react to it.

PREPARATION OF THE NEWS RELEASE

A good news release has several key parts:

1. **The headline.** For example, "XYZ CORPORATION FORMS A NEW JOINT VENTURE WITH GERMAN PARTNER." The headline should be in all caps and centered. It should also be as brief as possible and lead readers into the body of the release. The headline should also incorporate the shortest possible name for the company. Even though most companies have multi-word names that end in "Inc.," always use the shortest form of the name without the "Inc."

   Craft the shortest and most hard-hitting headline possible. The headline's job is to convey enough information about the news release that the reader will want to read more. Try to avoid the word "announces" in the headline. Don't say, "ABC announces a letter of intent to go public." Rather say, "ABC signs letter of intent to go public." The news release is the announcement.

2. **The dateline.** The dateline should include the city and state where the release is issued, usually the place where

the company is headquartered. Exceptions to this might be places where the company is doing business or is expecting to do business. Business editors always give preference to companies they consider local. The dateline also gives the full and official name of the company, specifies the exchange on which it trades, and identifies any particular index in which it is included.

3. **Body of the release.** The centerpiece of the news release is the information the company aims to disclose. For example, "John P. Jones, CEO of XYZ Corporation, has entered into an agreement with Munich-based Voxifone to form an R&D partnership . . . ."

The most important thing in the body of the news release is to make your point quickly and not dilute its content with meaningless information. Try to say what you need to in about 400 words or less, which is the length that editors look for in carrying stories.

There is some confusion about what comprises the 400 words. By the time companies add a standard tag line (of about 75 to 100 words) and a Safe Harbor statement, they can be near 400 words without having said anything of value. For this reason the story without these items must not exceed 400 words. The problem with the long disclaimers and tag lines is that the newswire services charge a flat fee for stories for the first 400 words; then they charge per word or per hundred words over that level.

If the release contains direct references to other companies (usually as customers), it is prudent to have the counsel of those companies approve the release. This is not absolutely necessary from a legal standpoint, as public companies are obliged to announce material news. However, companies must maintain good relations with their customers, and releasing news without their review could disrupt those relations. Few customers want the details of their contracts made public.

4. **Tag line and contact.** This short part of the news release provides a little information about the company, its Web URL, and the name and number that any new editor can call in following up on the story.

5. **Safe Harbor statement.** If your release contains forward-looking statements, it must include a Safe Harbor statement. All releases should be screened for forward-looking language. Anything that says what the company expects in the future should be construed as forward-looking and must be pointed to in a Safe Harbor statement at the end of the release. As mentioned in the chapter on disclosure, *do not automatically put a Safe Harbor disclaimer on all news releases.* This will cause the courts to view this as inoculation, and they could allow an attack on a legitimate statement as a result, making the Safe Harbor clause null and void. Point to the statement and cite specific risks of that statement.

    End all news releases with a triple pound sign (# # #) centered on the bottom of the page, as in the example news release (Figure 11–1). And *have a securities attorney check them* before they are actually made public.

THE DISTRIBUTION OF NEWS RELEASES

The same planning and focus that your company brings to advertising and promotion should be brought to the practice of distributing news releases. A blanket or "shotgun" approach to this function is not effective, efficient, or economical. Moreover, there are some regulatory restraints on when you can release announcements of material news.

The NASD

Within the NASD is a group commonly referred to as MarketWatch. Their task is to monitor the movement of stocks for sudden and large changes in price and/or volume. NASD MarketWatch is especially

FIGURE 11–1   Example News Release

FOR IMMEDIATE RELEASE

COMPANY HEADLINE

CITY, STATE, MONTH, DAY, YEAR—Company Name, Inc. (Nasdaq Small-Cap Market®: XXXX; Chicago Stock Exchange: XXX) announced that

Company President, Mr. Speak Goodly, said "xxxx xxxxxxx xxxxx."

Company Name, Inc. (www.xxxx.com) is a publicly traded company, formed in 19XX, to capitalize on emerging high-technology opportunities. World headquarters are in CITY, STATE.

Contact:
Mr. Speak Goodly
800-555-1212
XXX-FAX-XXXX Fax

Safe Harbor Statement under the Private Securities Litigation Reform Act of 1995

In accordance with the Safe Harbor provisions of the Private Securities Litigation Reform Act of 1995, the Company notes that statements in this press release, and elsewhere, that look forward in time, which include everything other than historical information, involve risks and uncertainties that may affect the Company's actual results of operations. The following important factors, among others that are discussed in company filings with the Securities and Exchange Commission, could cause actual results to differ materially from those set forth in the forward-looking statements:

[List relevant factors.]

# # #

---

vigilant about when and how material events are disclosed. This group has established a procedure for previewing the release of news or information that could affect a stock. During market trading hours, corporations are required to submit news releases to MarketWatch at least 10 minutes before distributing the news to the public. Normal market hours are weekdays from 9:30 A.M. to 4:00 P.M. eastern time. Premarket hours begin at 8:00 A.M. and postmarket hours continue to 6:30 P.M. eastern time.

You do not need to adhere to the lead-time rule when the market is closed, but you need to put out your news release at 20 minutes prior to the opening of the next trading session. When feasible, we recommend that all releases be distributed by 7:30 A.M. eastern time. This simplifies complying with the lead-time rule. Adhering to this policy, when feasible, means that those incidents or circumstances that do require news disclosure during trading hours will be critical, and therefore especially newsworthy: the death or resignation of a key executive, a disaster, a product recall, a hostile tender offer. In those cases, the NASD permits MarketWatch to be notified simultaneously with the announcement to the public. MarketWatch can be reached at **800-537-3929.** They can only accept *faxed* news releases at **240-386-6047.**

Your Main Constituents

Inform your market makers or your auction market specialist *directly* about the news simultaneously with its release to the general public. Always follow this procedure. Don't, however, provide advance word. You should also have an up-to-date file of your major investors' e-mail addresses over which you should transmit the release at the same time you release the news to the public.

News items for which the lead-time rule is waived are those that would be released over a major wire and distributed globally among all media outlets. The other material incident releases are just of interest to your shareholders, the investment community, your industrial peers, and the business press. You should maintain a file of the names and media contacts that should get these releases. This file should contain the media contacts for every town in which your company has employees. Don't overlook periodicals and newsletters that specialize or provide extensive coverage of your industry, your customers, and your suppliers.

The Investment Community

Two wire services provide distribution of news releases to the global securities markets: *P.R. Newswire* and *Business Newswire*. Your IR department should have established and maintained a first-name relationship with some account representatives at those companies. Your IR department should also make sure that they have transmitted any news release directly to any analyst or investment manager who has expressed an interest in your company but has not yet taken any action to support or purchase your stock. We recommend making a phone call to inform these prospective investors that you have done so. Some analysts and investment managers might receive as many as 500 releases or e-mails a day, and well over 2,000 in a week. Members of the investment community should be asked for their preferred method of being informed about material news. Their respective preferences should be in your IR contact database.

About Wire Services

Using a wire service should be standard IR practice. They are cost effective and efficient. The advantages are

- **Simultaneous delivery.** Wire services give simultaneous delivery of news, which keeps public companies away from selective-disclosure problems. This will also satisfy news dissemination problems encountered under Reg. FD.
- **Credibility.** Newly established companies can gain media recognition by utilizing quality wire services. These services lend greater credibility to potentially (or otherwise) unknown companies.

- **Distribution to all media.** Wire services generally distribute to all local print and broadcast media, all disclosure media, analysts, trade media, Internet sites and portals, and the wire's own Web site.

- **Efficient and cost effective.** Wire services are very time efficient. A client company need only make its distribution selections, determine the time of the release, and e-mail the document to the wire service. Wire services make nearly instantaneous and simultaneous releases via e-mail and fax to thousands of locations. It would cost a company a small fortune to replicate and maintain the equipment and personnel needed for this type of service.

- **Distribution to prominent organizations.** The only way to get news submitted to some of the more prominent Web-based news organizations (such as Yahoo!) is to submit it through an established wire service. Fraud protection is the motivation for this practice. Plus, wire services continually update the changing lists of submission points.

- **Hitting the right target audience.** The intended audience for the news release may be several or all of the following: journalists, analysts, investors, the Internet community, current or future customers, business partners, employees, or even competitors. (Yes, people who work for your competitors are potential buyers of your stock. They, more than others, can spot a profitable development announced via news release.) It may be limited to certain industries such as aerospace, banking, building and finance, chemicals, consumer and household, or energy. Also, company management may prefer anything from minimum to worldwide distribution of its release. The wire service can help with distribution based upon your criteria.

- **Distribution via trade wire.** Most major wire services also allow their clients to distribute for free to any pertinent trade wires. Trade wires are industry-specific wires that go primarily to publishers of trade-specific journals. These represent some of the best opportunities for actually getting a story published about a company. Most investors and the general public will never see these stories—but current and potential customers may very well see them.

- **International distribution.** Should you go global with your message? Most wire services can advise their clients on the feasibility of international distribution. Broader dissemination does not necessarily guarantee greater press coverage or stock buying. Companies with interests by shareholders abroad or with products and services that might have international appeal may have to consider broader (more expensive) distributions.

- **Translations.** Another major advantage of using a news wire for distribution is the translation feature. Even though English is the language of business in much of the world, many publications do not appreciate the cavalier approach of a single-language distribution. With so much news to pick from, the easiest thing for an editor to do is to eliminate news releases that require translation.

   If you are distributing anything in Canada, a French translation is mandatory. We have had many Canadian clients that could translate the news release themselves but prefer to wait for the wire distribution translation.

- **Proofreaders provided.** No matter how well a news release has been developed and gone over, small mistakes can slip through. It is important to have a fresh pair of eyes make one last review of the document before it is sent out. Most wire services have two people review copy before it is finally released.

- **Of format and hot links.** Wire services will put your news release into a standard press format (such as an Associated Press format). They also hot link items in the release for the electronic version so that recipients can easily locate referenced material.

- **Authorized agents.** Another advantage to wire services is that changes can only be made by authorized persons. Be aware that there have been instances in which unscrupulous people have made false news releases through a company's wire service. Ask your wire service what safeguards are in place to prevent just such an occurrence.

WORKING WITH A WIRE SERVICE

Wire services offer a broad range of services. These can make your IR department chores less onerous and ensure that mandated disclosure requirements are met. A company can get the most out of these services if it understands how to work effectively with its wire service providers.

Distribution Arrangements

Client companies can upload, store, and utilize their e-mail and fax distribution lists. In this way a company can specify to send their news release (and to which list(s)) at the same time as they place each release with their wire service for distribution. This service offers convenience and is a safeguard to be sure the distribution went out as well as a way to stop all distributions if there is a change of plans. Also, clients can be certain that the same draft is going to everyone. The wire service can monitor the distribution to meet existing rules and regulations.

Confirming Faxes

Faxes can be useful because the e-mail version does not always go through. If the last thing you did on Friday night was to e-mail out a news release to the wire service for Monday morning distribution, but your server (or the other side's server) was down, you wouldn't even know that it failed to go through until Monday morning. Most wire services will call when they have received your e-mailed version.

Be Available

Be sure that the wire service can reach someone in authority between the time you send your news release and the time it is set for distribution. If they find an error, they will either hold up your distribution or you risk something else going wrong. Always provide contact information on a 24-hour basis.

Know the Whereabouts of Your Sources

It is important is to have access to any of your sources for a news release on the same basis (as listed above) prior to news being released. Wire services run 24 hours a day, 7 days a week; so if the release needs to be pulled at the last minute, this can be done easily.

Password-Protected Submissions

Most wire services will allow you to submit your release to their Web site via password protection. When submitting a news release, a company always gives its account number, which is generally sufficient for security reasons.

Visual Elements

Visual elements such as photos, logos, graphics and graphic illustrations, streaming video, and audio can be linked to your story. They can be added to stories and stored on the Web for access by major news services for up to a year for one flat fee.

Crossing the Wire

Wire services call and confirm the time that your news was released to the public—this is known as "crossing the wire." The IR manager can check the status of a release by looking for company news on sites such as Yahoo.com, CNBC.com, and Quicken.com.

Unfortunately, some members of the brokerage community fail to pick up releases because they are on archaic systems that only pick up news from one of the wire feed services, such as Dow or Reuters. These news wire feeds nearly always pick up quarterly and annual financial results as well as bad news or scandals. They are not paid services (at least not by the companies making the releases), so they are not obligated to pick up anything. They are looking for their own definition of news. This definition varies with the time of year.

News Congestion

Not all the news gets through when a lot of financial reporting is taking place. Companies must report their annual results within 90 days of their year-end. They must report their quarterly results within 45 days of the end of each quarter (fourth quarter excepted). As most companies end their years on December 31, they must report their annual results by March 31, their first quarter by May 15, their second quarter by August 15, and their third quarter by November 15. The two-week period leading up to the quarterly filings and four-week period leading up to the annual filings tend to be very busy times for these wire feeds.

As They Like It

It is very important that your news is distributed in ways that meet the preferences of your audience, whether that is by fax or e-mail. Also, be sure to give your recipients the option on each correspondence to have their names *removed* from your distribution lists. This may be done as easily as just giving a fax back, e-mail back, or phone option to deal with these changes.

Getting Distribution beyond the Wire

The press is always looking for experts to quote. They typically want quotations from at least three sources for any story. This demand creates an opportunity to obtain greater visibility for the company. The major wire services now offer opportunities to present people from a company as experts to the press. Some firms charge extra for this service, others do not. Media exposure is invaluable if a higher profile within your industry, community, or the financial community is desired.

Payment Options

Wire services offer several payment options. A client can pay the bill directly or through its PR or IR agency. Even when paying directly, the client company can still authorize its agency to make release decisions on its behalf and have the bill charged to them directly.

TRACKING THE NEWS

Getting the news out is just one of the IR manager's chores. Tracking the news as it appears is another. News tracking serves two important purposes:

1. It allows company executives to know what is being said about them to investors, customers, and the general public. If the company or its representatives are being inaccurately quoted or inappropriately described, senior management should know about it and take corrective measures.

2. It helps company decision makers develop a more complete view of their competitors, important trends, and how they fit into the competitive landscape.

Print and Web Tracking

For more than 100 years, the only way to track news was with traditional or hard-copy press clipping services. Human readers scanned thousands of publications for specified search criteria.

Once items were found, they were clipped, captioned, sorted, and mailed to clients. These traditional services continue to be a popular source for capturing the traditional clip. However, the lag time between publication date and the client's receipt of clippings has created a need for gathering information quicker.

Lag times disappeared in the 1990s with the introduction of electronic clipping services. Instead of the two- to four-day lags, clippings are now delivered within minutes of when they are released electronically. Coverage by these electronic clippers typically includes print publications such as newspapers, magazines, trade journals, and wire services. Clients outline the type of news that they deem important. The search criteria can, in fact, be very precise. The services then automatically deliver matching articles by e-mail or post them to a password-protected Web site.

Electronic clipping services are the perfect tool for instant updates of important news. However, print is not the only news medium that needs to be monitored. The Internet has emerged as another important source.

News watchers began tracking the World Wide Web in the mid-1990s for reported company rumors in bulletin boards, e-mail discussion groups, and public forums.

In the late 1990s, the Internet experienced an explosion of on-line news outlets, such as latimes.com, nytimes.com, techweb.com, and thestreet.com. Major daily newspapers, trades, and business publications now host on-line versions of their print publications. The Internet has also given birth to the e-zine, or Internet/on-line-only publication.

The Internet news explosion has also spawned Internet clipping services, which typically offer three types of Internet monitoring: news, newsgroups, and public areas. These services search several thousand news sites, and can read more than a million articles each day. They track as many as 63,000 newsgroups and visit thousands of corporate, government, and education sites on the Internet. Users receive notification via e-mail or Web site delivery with abstracts containing their search criteria and hyperlinks directly to the sites where their coverage appears.

Advanced technology now offers users improved search capabilities. Users can make their searches as precise or as simple as they wish. Technology ensures that old content is weeded out, delivering users only the freshest news mentions on the Web. The Internet-monitoring service compares the search criteria to what it finds on the Internet. Each time a match is found, it is added to a notification report that is sent to a user usually once a day by e-mail. The notification includes the headline of each story, posting, or mention, an extract containing the key search criteria, and the hyperlink that allows the user to go directly to the site where the information appeared.

Some services offer Web delivery, archiving, and clipping management capabilities.

Broadcast Monitoring

The newest service designed to keep tabs on news coverage is a broadcast monitoring service. Mentions from news broadcasts are now available within an hour of actual broadcast! Broadcast services provide all stories that mention the search criteria specified by the client. Stories are sorted by broadcast networks, cable networks, date, market, and station. Some services include the number of viewers and the value of the mention. Typically, clients can see the text of the mention within an hour of the actual broadcast and, if they need it, a video clip that can be delivered within 24 hours.

QUICK RESULTS

These monitoring services offer quick results without hassle. They make it easy for companies to follow their own news, keep tabs on competitors, watch targeted industries, and monitor the impact of their public relations campaigns. Most services require no hardware, software, or training, and are fairly priced.

Local and Regional Media

Your IR head should have an established relationship with the business news editors of your local and regional media. Do not underestimate the level of interest they have in your company. Your company is a local employer and purchaser of locally purveyed goods and services. The growth of your company enhances the local economy, which has a direct impact on advertising revenues. These editors and news directors have great degrees of flexibility in the timing and the placement of news items. They can be strong allies in your total corporate communications campaign. It is not best practice, but the only practice to ensure that they get news about your company as soon as anyone. Make a practice of providing "scoops" when you have some new information that is interesting but not deemed material.

Public Relations Agencies

Press and media coverage about your company enjoys the greatest degree of credibility about your stock's investment appeal. A public relations agency can be one of your most effective allies in raising the investing public's interest in your company, or retaining the wrong agency can be a severe waste of money. Don't hire any agency until you have completed a due diligence study. Some of the points to be checked in the study are

1. How long has the agency been in business?
2. How many clients do they have who have been clients for three years or more?
3. Is the agency willing to refer you to all their clients?
4. Has the agency ever been accused of misrepresentation or any other kind of malfeasance? Are they aware of disclosure regulations, most notably SEC Reg. FD?
5. What is the average length of employment among the account executives?

6. What is their reputation among the media: local, regional, and national?

7. What services and assistance can they provide: preparing press releases, scheduling conferences, preparing media kits, etc.?

8. What are terms that govern how the agency is compensated?

One of the key issues in choosing an agency is the manner in which they assisted and/or advised clients on handling material news that was bad news.

FOLLOWING UP

A procedural outline should be in place for determining what resulted from your news release.

Monitor not only the change in your stock price but also the changes in volume. The response of the market to the news may not be immediate. Stay alert to any significant changes in price and volume.

Calls from investors, brokers, or the media triggered by the release should be recorded. Include in the record the date, time, identification of the caller, and a summary of the call's key elements. If a caller's question indicates that you did not provide all the relevant information about that particular material event, then issue a release addressing those specific queries.

The real value of retaining a clipping service or Internet monitor is realized in that period following the release of material news. You can ascertain the scope of interest in your company by the number of mentions these services garner and forward to you.

THE PRESS KIT

Other than news releases, there is other printed communication that the effective IR program prepares. Two of the most common print items are the *Fact Sheet* and the *Executive Summary*. These two items are usually combined with the most recent news releases and the latest 10-K and 10-Q report to make up what is generally referred to as a *press kit*. A press kit is assembled for distribution to anyone who requests information about the company. Brochures describing a company's products and/or services may also be included. The information included in the executive summary and in the fact sheet are sufficient, when combined with the latest 10-K and 10-Q, to provide a point of departure for a due-diligence study of your company.

Fact Sheet

A fact sheet is no more than a list of talking points and is generally formatted in a column of bulleted points. It should contain only information that has been previously disclosed. Do not use this form of print presentation to disclose new material information. The bullet format is employed because the fact sheet is often used as a talking-point outline for phone calls to brokers or the media. The order of talking points is

1. Name of the company.
2. Single sentence about what the company does.
3. The company's competitive advantage.
4. Where the company's stock is listed and its symbol.
5. Key material information that makes the stock attractive.
6. Shares outstanding and the float.
7. Market cap.
8. Name of brokers who are following the stock. plus three or four points about the reasons why the stock appeals to existing shareholders.

Executive Summary

The executive summary is similar in scope and format to reports prepared by brokerage analysts.

It differs from an analyst's report in that

1. It contains no buy or sell recommendation.
2. It provides no performance targets.
3. It has no risk disclosure section.

The length of the executive summary should be no longer than four pages, the usual dimensions of which are 8½-by-11 inches. The format that we recommend is presented in Appendix 11–A.

Again, do not disclose any new material information in an executive summary. By including a Safe Harbor statement within the executive summary, though, you can make appropriate forward-looking statements.

Nevertheless, we recommend not including forward-looking statements as a best practice. Compliance officials at many broker/dealer firms prohibit their brokers from sending clients and prospects any literature that includes forward-looking statements.

THE NEXT CHAPTER

The next chapter reviews the best practices of the other two significant activities that characterize a professional IR program. Group presentations and conference calls are considered by some professional investors to be of greater importance than news releases.

Our Sample Executive Summary Format

COMPANY NAME
MONTH–2001

Executive Summary

Description:	Description of the company's business—a sentence or short statement.
Traded:	Nasdaq (or the Exchange where it is listed).
Symbol:	The stock and warrant symbols.
Manuals:	Standard and Poor's (or Moody's).
Shares Outstanding:	Total shares currently outstanding.
Float:	All of the shares that are available for public trading—not part of the restricted shares. Restricted shares include all 144 shares that are not yet available for sale, including the shares of the officers, directors, and control persons (those that own more than 10 percent of the outstanding shares).
Transfer Agent:	The name of the transfer agent and the city and state where they are located.

Executive Summary (*continued*)

Accountant:	The name of the accounting firm.
Corporate Address:	The address of the public company.
Recent Price:	$ bid—Quote the bid as of the date of the report and show the date.
Trading Range:	$–$—Show the price range for the past 12 months.
Revenue Year-End:	$—Show the revenue from the last year-end number. Compliance officers like to see this on the front page.
Assets:	$—We usually show the most recent number from the 10-Q and date the number.
Liabilities:	$—We usually show the most recent number from the 10-Q and date the number.
Equity:	$—We usually show the most recent number from the 10-Q and date the number.
Book Value per Share:	$—We usually show the most recent number from the 10-Q and date the number.
Employs:	The number of employees.
Fiscal Year:	The date of the fiscal year-end.

Note: Any changes or notes

Business Summary

The business summary should be one to three paragraphs long. State in a simple and concise manner the basic business plan of the company. Explain the company's advantages or competitive edge(s) in its market segment.

Industry

Give a brief description of the industry in which the company competes. The total size of the industry should be stated as well as the industry growth rate. Detail the number of competitors and the company's current share of this industry.

Customers

Include the total number of customers and name the prominent ones in bulleted form. A list of customers is an opportunity for small, unrecognized companies to gain credibility. We call it "borrowing the credibility of others." The fact that a small company has large customers is a tacit endorsement of its products and services.

History

Lay out the company's history as a series of milestone events. Each milestone need only contain a one- to three-sentence description.

Month, Year—Founded

Month, Year—Incorporated

Month, Year—Began sales

Month, Year—First profitable year

Month, Year—Sales milestone

Month, Year—First patent

Month, Year—Second patent

Month, Year—Other significant events

Month, Year—Became public

Month, Year—Sales milestone

Month, Year—Large new customer added

Background

Provide a short narrative describing the background that gave birth to the company and its original and ensuing concepts. The background section should answer the following questions:

- Was this company conceived as an outgrowth of another company or started from scratch?

- Who began the company, and when did they begin it?
- Why was it started?
- Did the founders see a market niche that had not been exploited?
- Was there more demand for these services than companies able to deliver services?
- Why was the company able to compete efficiently for customers?
- How was it originally funded?
- Who funded it? Are they still involved today? What are their plans as far as remaining with the company?

Products and Services

Answer the following questions:

- What are the company's products or services?
- Why are the company's products or services important in their market space?
- How many products or services does the company have?
- What percentage of sales does each of these products or services constitute?
- What products or services does the company foresee in its future?
- How important are these new products?
- What competitive edges will they bring?
- Will they open up new markets?
- Will they address existing problems? If so, how?
- Will they displace existing products?
- Will the new products have any competition?
- How will these products or services be marketed?

Financial

Create a condensed summary of the most recent balance sheet and income statements from the current quarter and the most recent annual report. This should contain a condensed version of the Management's Discussion and Analysis and/or management's comments from the most recent financial news release describing results.

Management

This section should detail the top three to six management people. Each manager should have a detailed paragraph. It should describe

- Their jobs held.
- Their duties and responsibilities.
- The number of people they supervise in total.
- The size of their budget responsibilities.
- Major accomplishments. (If they don't have any accomplishments, an investor will wonder why they should invest in an unproven commodity.)

Current Developments

Use this section to describe a recent contract award or some other recent milestone event(s): one to three separate items.

Future Expectations

If there is a contract pending or a new product about to be launched, discuss it in a paragraph. Do this in a nonspecific manner without any guidance or performance objectives.

Conclusions

In a bulleted list, in descending order from most to least importance, give 10 to 15 reasons why someone should consider buying shares of this company. Each bulleted item can be one to three sentences long.

Include a typical disclaimer if the report is prepared by an outside agency.

The author of this report is not a Registered Investment Advisor or a broker/dealer. The content of this report is provided as an information service only, and past performance of previously featured companies does not guarantee the future success of any company. Information contained herein is based upon data obtained from the Company, as well as other recognized statistical services, issuer reports, communications, or other sources believed to be reliable. Sources include interviews with management, news releases, and Forms 10-KSB and 10-QSB. However, such information has not been verified, and we make no representation to its accuracy or completeness. Any statements nonfactual in nature constitute only current opinions that are subject to change. Our company, its officers, directors, and employees may have positions in securities referred to in this report, and may from time to time buy or sell these positions. Neither the information nor any opinion expressed shall be construed to be or constitute an offer to buy any securities mentioned herein. This report was prepared for compensation [*state the amount of compensation*], which may have been any combination of cash or securities. This report does not purport to be a complete statement of all data relevant to the securities mentioned. Use of the information provided is at the sole risk of the investor, and neither the author, associates, shareholders, or employees/consultants accept any liability whatsoever for any direct or consequential loss that may arise from any use of this report or its contents. These securities may involve a high degree of risk. These securities may be considered speculative and therefore not suitable for the strictly conservative investor. Forward-looking statements involving any representations other than historical fact involve risks and uncertainties that would cause outcomes to differ from projections. Receipt of this report shall not create, under any circumstances, any implication that there has been no change in the affairs of the company profiled. Any readers of this report who are considering purchasing securities mentioned herein should consult their own financial advisors prior to making any investment decision. The author further urges readers of this report who are considering investing in the company to check its filings with the Securities and Exchange Commission (SEC) on the SEC's EDGAR Web site.

[If you use any forward-looking statements, a statement similar to the following should be included. As per our disclosure chapter (see Chapter 8), the risks need to refer to the specific statements that are forward-looking in nature.]

Safe Harbor Statement under the Private Securities Litigation Reform Act of 1995

In accordance with the Safe Harbor provisions of the Private Securities Litigation Reform Act of 1995, the Company notes that statements made herein, that look forward in time, which include everything other than historical information, involve risks and uncertainties that may affect its actual results of operations. The following important factors, among others that are discussed in company filings with the Securities and Exchange Commission, could cause actual results to differ materially from those set forth in the forward-looking statements:

[List relevant factors.]

CHAPTER 12

Best Practices for Conference Calls and Presentations

NOT SURPRISINGLY, PRINTED INFORMATION does not have as immediate an impact on the price of your stock as oral communication has. Even less surprising is that conversations or personal presentations are the most likely opportunities to get into disclosure trouble. The limited audience precludes disclosing material information for the first time. Our "breath-holding" exercises are always done during teleconferences and presentations. Analysts, experienced investors, and media professionals are masters at prompting you to divulge everything that is material, or soon could be material. They aren't violating any regulations by asking questions. The aggravation they may exhibit when you cite Reg. FD pales in considerable degree to the response you will get from the SEC.

Be ever mindful.

If you inadvertently do disclose new information that could be deemed material, have some company colleague inform the SEC within 10 minutes, and distribute a general news release within 20 minutes. File an 8-K report with the SEC within 3 hours. You have probably broken up your teleconference or presentation, another unfortunate consequence of your slip of the tongue.

Be ever mindful.

If you plan to disclose new information in a teleconference or presentation, disclose it in a general news release shortly before the scheduled call or address. If you are going to do this during market hours, remember the NASD MarketWatch requirement. Again, this NASD stricture is why we urge our clients not to schedule presentations or teleconferences during market trading hours.

Be ever mindful.

THE TELECONFERENCE (aka THE CONFERENCE CALL)

A not easily exasperated microcap-portfolio manager remarked to us, "I've never participated in a conference call that I thought was conducted in an appropriate and efficient way." She was talking about scores of teleconferences conducted by companies just like yours. Reg. FD has greatly complicated the conducting of effective conference calls. In theory, a company cannot limit participation. In practice, the logistical challenges imposed by Reg. FD on arranging conference calls have moved administrative and support staff to tears. The best practices for complying with the onerous burdens of Reg. FD are still evolving.

You *must outline a structure* to follow throughout the conference call. You need to stick to that outline up to the time when you open the conference to questions from callers. Sticking to the outline ensures that you will stay focused and that you will not disclose any new material information. A conference call is the most appropriate channel in which to make forward-looking statements; therefore, always begin a conference call by reading a Safe Harbor statement.

Scheduling a Conference Call

The best practice with respect to how often to schedule a conference call is four times a year. The calls should be conducted to address the issues reported in the most recent 10-K or 10-Q. The date of the call should be on the same day these reports are sent to the SEC and the new release summarizing the information in the report has been distributed.

Send the reports to the SEC and distribute the news release five minutes after the close of trading hours. Schedule the conference call for 10 minutes later. Announce the date and time of the scheduled conference call at least three days preceding the day on which you will be hosting that conference call. The best days for conference calls are Tuesday through Thursday. We know of companies who distributed their 10-Q or 10-K news release after the Friday close of trading. Their intent was to curry favor by allowing people weekend time to prepare for a Monday morning conference call. This is not smart. There is the chance that many people might not see the Friday release and will be angry with your company for putting them at a supposed disadvantage. Again, schedule your conference calls in the middle of the week after trading hours and within minutes of distributing 10-Q or 10-K news releases.

Conducting the Conference Call

The CEO should be the featured speaker. The meeting should open with someone reading directly from a written form of the Safe Harbor statement. The CEO then takes the phone and introduces the other executives from the company who will participate in the call. There should be no more than three other senior officers, including the CFO.

The CEO should then spend no more than five minutes summarizing the recently disclosed material information upon which the call is focused. After doing that, the CEO makes only those forward-looking statements that *have been scripted*. The other senior managers should then have no more than five minutes to comment or elaborate on the previous comments.

Then open the proceedings for questions. Repeat each question before addressing it. Be sure that the people asking the questions identify themselves and their affiliations. Answer each question succinctly. Always defer the answer to the company executive on the call who is best informed on the matter in question. If you or someone else can't answer the question, say so immediately and be precise about why you can't answer. Keep the call going until there are no more questions. Close the call by thanking the callers for their time and *their interest in your company*.

Two of the most common questions asked during a conference call deal with *daily sales outstanding* ("dso's") and how companies treat deferred revenues. Be ever mindful.

Conference Call Follow-Up

Within two days of a conference call, brokers, analysts, and invest-ment managers who phoned in for that call should be contacted for their evaluation of the call. These follow-up calls should be made by your IR head. The IR head should have established enough regard among or rapport with these professionals to get honest, candid responses. You should respect the confidence he or she has to maintain with investment professionals. The reason for the follow-up is to get a "constructive" critique of the CEO but also to learn how to make the next call better in every way.

PRESENTATIONS AND ROAD SHOWS

Live presentations to groups of shareholders and interested inves-tors have the most immediate impact on the price of your stock than any other form of communication. Live presentations are held outside the company offices more frequently than on the company premises. Many are conducted away from the town in which your company's headquarters are located. These presenta-tions are commonly called *road shows*. The following discussion on best practice procedures applies to both road shows and local presentations.

It may be useful to begin this section with the case of a com-pany CEO who broke *all* the rules of effective presentations in one presentation, something we had never seen before or since. It was a memorable performance. This CEO deluged his audience with information. But once he finished, members of the audience (all experienced retail brokers) approached us to ask what the company did. We told them in about three sentences what the company did and then gave them three reasons to care. Their response was, "Why didn't he just say that?"

Although we had written an entire outline for this particular presentation, our client ignored it. As the CEO of a small telecommunications company (he had been a key executive with a Fortune 500 corporation), he was sure that he knew more about doing broker presentations than we did. And though he had never been in a position to sell this or any other company to the investment community, he was quite certain that he had the right angle for approaching this audience.

Reading from his own prepared script, our client talked over the heads of the attending brokers, and he droned on, using impenetrable jargon, about all the mundane details of his business even as he failed to impart relevant information. He lost his audience within the first few minutes without even realizing it. It was truly one of the most embarrassing presentations we have ever observed.

If this client broke all the rules of good presentations, what are those rules? In our definition, a good investor presentation runs between 15 and 30 minutes (not counting the question-and-answer portion) and uses 30 to 40 slides. If management cannot articulate a case for owning its shares within that time, it generally cannot make the case at all. If the audience is mostly brokers, their interest falls off exponentially as the presentation stretches beyond 15 minutes. If it goes past 30 minutes, all will have lost interest.

Besides being brief, a good presentation has these characteristics:

- Clear explanation of what the company does.
- Effective slides.
- Logical format.

- Clear transitions.
- Good delivery.
- Information that is relevant for the audience.
- Free of jargon.
- Long enough to cover the material but no longer—clarity pays.
- Well-rehearsed.

Now, let's consider each in detail.

Clear Explanation of What the Company Does

Every presentation should begin with a clear and concise explanation of what the company does. The speaker should be able to do this in just a few brief paragraphs. A surprising number of presenters fail to observe this simple and seemingly obvious requirement. The authors have been to several presentations at which the spokesperson assumed that the audience knew what the company did and never once explained it to them. This is extremely irritating to attendees.

Effective Slides

Fewer words create bigger impact. Each slide should contain the talking point for the speaker during the next 30 to 60 seconds.

Think of a slide as you would the heading in a news release. It should arouse interest and make the reader want to know more. A slide is not the story and should not be used to tell the story—that is the speaker's job. A slide merely underscores a point that the speaker is making.

Logical Format

Every presentation must follow a logical format. Facts and insight presented in a logical fashion help to convince and create acceptance.

Presentation planning and outlining—with plenty of outside critique—is the best way to create a logical format.

Clear Transitions

How many presentations have you attended at which the speaker jumped erratically from subject to subject? When transitioning from one subject to the next, it is important to set the stage by introducing the next subject and show its connection to what went before.

Speakers who jump from one subject to the next without clear transitions lose their audiences in at least two ways:

1. Many in the audience will not realize that the subject has changed and will be left wondering how the two different concepts are related.

2. The confused audience will tune out the new material for a moment.

Slides can be used to announce new subjects—if they are used properly. Do not talk ahead or behind the subject on the current slide.

Good Delivery

Presentations should be made with enthusiasm and energy. Enthusiasm sells. Use stories when you can, as they draw the listeners in. When describing difficult concepts, make analogies to familiar concepts and circumstances. Make it as easy to relate to these things as possible.

There are two things to avoid when making live oral presentations. Never put the entire copy in front of the audience and then read the slide to them. This is demeaning and insults their intelligence. They can read for themselves. It is okay to list bullet items and use them as your talking points. Do not just read everything to them verbatim.

The other item to avoid is making any presentation that sounds as though you are reading from a script. This is a huge annoyance to the audience and makes the speaker seem ignorant and boring. A presentation should seem so natural that the audience is never aware that the presenter is reading from a script, if the presenter is even doing so. The audience expects the speaker to have intimate knowledge of the subject, to speak with authority and knowledge, and not to deliver a "canned" presentation. This is a difficult tightrope to walk and may sound like conflicting advice — practice but don't sound "canned."

Keeping and Losing the Audience

Some speakers lose their audiences without realizing it. There are several ways this happens and several signs that it is happening. The most common is adding irrelevant content. More is *not* better. There is always plenty of relevant information to convey without adding the irrelevant. By adding information beyond the scope of the audience's interest a spokesperson risks losing the attention of the audience. Some members of the audience will tolerate this out of pure politeness, but not for long.

A speaker should watch for signs that the audience is tuning out: side conversations, people not watching the presentation, tapping of pencils on tabletops, etc. Each is a sign that the speaker has lost, or is losing, the audience. Some speakers try to recapture the audience by talking faster. This will generally lose the audience faster. The best method to draw the audience back is with a story or an anecdote.

Provisions of Only Relevant Information

To a CEO, every detail of the business is tremendously important, and some make the mistake of trying to cover everything. An audience of investors, however, has a narrow window of attention and specific interests. Therefore, the CEO, or other presenter, must first think through the following questions: Who is my audience? What do they want to know? Answering these questions can help the speaker determine what is relevant and what is not.

A good company spokesperson tells the audience what they want to know—not what the speaker wants to tell them. Knowing the audience and understanding their needs is the first step in creating a productive presentation. The next step is to know what you want to convey.

Free of Jargon

Some people believe that jargon makes them sound intelligent. In fact, the heavy use of jargon in a presentation actually makes the spokesperson appear arrogant and intentionally talking over the heads of listeners. Jargon interferes with communication—so don't use it.

De-"jargonizing" a presentation or a business plan is the single best reason to hire outside IR counsel. We were once hired by a public company from New York that had a business plan developed by a local investor relations firm. They sent us this plan and asked us to consult with them, as they were seeking market support and funding but were getting nowhere.

After reading the business plan, we told them that we didn't understand what it was that they did. They were shocked. When we asked them what a "CLEC" was, they questioned whether we were the right people for the job. "Everyone in our industry understands CLEC," we were told. Our response was direct, the fact that we *don't* know what a CLEC is meant that we were perfect for the job! "Are you trying to sell this business plan to people in your industry?" we asked. They said, "No, of course not."

Eventually, they came to understand that if we could not understand the language of their business plan, other people were likely having the same trouble.

Clarity Pays

The jargon problem just described is fairly typical of presentations and business plans. That particular plan never addressed the basic questions:

- What is the nature of the business?
- Where were they in their plan?
- Where were they headed?
- How did they plan to get there?

The client eventually realized the wisdom of approaching the plan through these questions and agreed to have us write an executive summary. In doing so we disregarded their original business plan. We conducted long-distance phone interviews with management, listened to their story, asked questions, retold them the story we were hearing, and constantly refined the writing.

The final result was a 2,500-word executive summary. The client took that summary to their investment banker, who reportedly remarked, "Thank God! We now, for the first time, understand what it is that you are trying to accomplish. We always thought there was something here, but we were never sure what it was." This banker gave the client his commitment to raise $65 million.

Well Rehearsed

No one has the talent to make a great, unrehearsed presentation. A good speaker will rehearse a presentation several times, using a parallel list of the slides with a subset of talking points that he or she does not want to miss. Reading the presentation aloud several times has the following benefits:

1. Sets the ideas into the spokesperson's mind.
2. Allows the presenter to hear problems ahead of the actual presentation and to make script adjustments.
3. Sets the timing of the presentation.

4. Avoids the poor reception that usually accompanies impromptu presentations.

Different Presentations for Different Audiences

It is not unusual to develop a slightly different presentation for different audiences—that is, a different *slant*. A slant is a variation on a story. Like using a resume—to different types of employers, a story can be made to fit different audiences. Here's an example.

If we were going to pitch an environmental fund (a green fund), we would emphasize our client's environmental benefits. If we were to pitch a sector fund, we would try to draw the most positive comparisons between our company and its peer group. If we were pitching to a retail broker audience, we would spend more time on the story aspects of the presentation. In pitching to an analyst, we would take a more numbers-oriented approach.

Investors want to know:

- What is the name of the company?
- What does the company do?
- What is the company's (almost) unfair advantage in the marketplace?
- Where did the company come from (its background and history)?
- Where is the company today (financials and current product or service sales)?
- Where is the company going (financially and/or product and service sales)?
- Why should they care?

A Model PowerPoint Presentation

Microsoft's PowerPoint is the industry standard for presentation graphics. Every IR professional should know how to make clear and compelling overheads with it. We suggest the following basic outline for every PowerPoint presentation:

- Begin with a Title Slide—this should contain nothing but the company's name and/or logo. Slogans are optional.
- Bullet point a summary of the "reasons to care" about the company—usually three to five reasons.
- Explain what the company does. Ideally this should be articulated in a single sentence. Then expand on what the company does and fully articulate the message with as many slides as necessary.
- Indicate what makes the company unique.
  - What selling advantages does it have?
  - What competitive advantages does it have?
  - What are its unique products or services?
  - What are the bars to entry?
- Management is next. Identify the key people and briefly discuss what is special about them.
- Market background and history. Briefly indicate how the company started and what led to the development of its business concept.
- Bullet the corporate milestones:
  - The year founded.
  - The year incorporated.
  - First year of revenues.
  - Patents received, and when.
  - Major employee milestones attained.
  - Sales milestones.
- Current status and financials.
- Where is the company at the present time (on its planned path)?

- Current products or services offered.

- Balance sheet.

- Income statement.

- The future:

  - What new products and services does the company plan to add or delete?

  - Expected growth in revenue and net income.

- Why should the audience care? This is management's chance to tell the audience why they should be shareholders.

- Summary.

- Review the opening (slide) of the three to five hottest reasons to own the company's shares.

- Any new or horizon events to look for. Give an idea of timing and management's expectation of the possibility of these events happening.

- Add concluding comments that tie up loose ends or add to the wrap-up section—for example, how you hope the shareholders will be rewarded.

Increasing Retention

Even if you made a great presentation, count yourself lucky if the audience retains 30 percent of what you've doled out. To increase retention, presenters need to

- Limit the number of points.

- Clearly explain the relevance of each point.

- Make key points in different ways to accommodate different learning styles.

- Appeal to as many of the senses as possible.

MEETINGS LIMITED TO
INVESTMENT PROFESSIONALS

Live presentations and meetings restricted to brokers, analysts, and institutional investors need to be conducted differently from meetings attended by individual investors. These meetings will even differ from one another if your company restricts meetings to just one of these groups. Brokers hear and behave in substantially and significantly different ways from analysts and institutional investors.

Broker Meetings

Broker meetings should take place after market hours, and always serve drinks and hors d'oeuvres. Not serving these things is considered rude, and affects attendance and future attitudes about the company. Broker attendance at these meetings is not mandatory from their standpoint. In fact, they are doing the company a favor by attending, so be a good host and show them some appreciation by buying them a drink and giving them some food. You would do no less for someone that you invite to your home.

We recommend that these meetings begin about half an hour after the markets close. The meeting location should be convenient for invitees, and free parking is always a plus. Remember that the goal is to encourage attendance.

Tuesday, Wednesday, and Thursday are the best days for broker meetings and for the same reason cited above for conference calls.

Meetings tend to be small (20 to 30 brokers or analysts), intimate affairs, and can cost the company more than $4,000 per meeting. The company must also bear the cost of travel, invitations, brokerage lists, postage, someone calling through the list of invitees, confirmation calls, food and drinks, material preparation, fax reminders, and follow-up calls after the meeting to assess the company's performance.

To extend the number of presentations given in any particular city, we suggest lunch-time broker meetings in brokerage firm offices. Nearly every firm of any size (30 brokers or more) has conference room facilities. We have had tremendous success at making presentations in these facilities while brokers (and support staff) eat lunches provided by our client companies. This approach eliminates the cost of renting a meeting room. Ordering sandwiches from a local shop is a fraction of the price of hors d'oeuvres and drinks served in a hotel meeting room. Best of all, attendance is close to 100 percent. In summary, this approach creates top-of-mind awareness during market hours at very little cost.

Want Fries with That Order?

We were once hired to introduce a new, double-drive-through hamburger chain to the retail broker market. The concept was relatively new and unknown at the time. We saw this as an opportunity to accomplish two objectives at once: create product PR for the client while conducting our IR project at a minimum cost.

Our approach was simple. We had two large insulated food containers made up with the company's logo. Meanwhile, we set noon appointments on separate days at every second-tier (on down) brokerage office in Denver. We called in advance, made appointments, and got head counts. On the appointed days we brought in burgers, chicken sandwiches, spicy fries, and soft drinks for the entire office. While the brokers sampled the goods, we described the advantages of the double-drive-through-burger concept.

The campaign was a huge success. Within 90 days, more than 400 brokers knew the company's story, and had direct experience with its products.

Group versus Individual Meetings

Whenever we have a client on a road trip, we try to schedule both individual meetings and group presentations. There are two reasons for this. First, you only have two time slots for group meetings: a noon meeting in a brokerage firm office and a meeting after market hours. Second, some audiences are better handled in a group and others are better handled as individuals.

We find that brokers prefer to attend group meetings. These meetings have a social element, as most of the brokers in a city know each other. Also, a group dynamic can emerge from such meetings. Brokers tend to follow one another. If they perceive that a successful broker is interested in a company, others will follow.

We have found that brokers generally do not like one-on-one meetings for the following reasons:

- They do not like the pressure of having a meeting devoted exclusively to them (they feel that this makes them more accountable to the issuer).
- They like the flexibility of coming to the meeting if and when they have time.
- They like to be able to leave when they want to.

Meetings with Investment Managers and Analysts

Institutional investors, however, want only one-on-one meetings. They expect a tailored presentation. They like to be able to interrupt with questions and take the conversation in different directions, depending upon their interests and knowledge.

THE NEXT CHAPTER

There are three areas of corporate strategy, the execution of which will determine how experienced investors will value your company in the short term. We examine them in Chapter 13.

Corporate Strategy and Market Value: The Three Areas Where Actions Speak the Loudest

W E HAVE DISCUSSED WHY, HOW, AND TO WHOM you demonstrate and communicate your commitment to increasing the value of your company. In this chapter, we discuss how certain decisions and tactics are *perceived* by shareholders and investors. There are three areas in which actions override anything you could say or disclose. These areas of corporate activity have as great an impact on market capitalization as increases in earnings and free cash flow. The three strategic areas that experienced investors will examine closely once they take an initial interest in your company are executive compensation, derivative financing, and mergers and acquisitions. Executive compensation and mergers and acquisitions are areas treated extensively by Alfred Rappaport in his bestselling *Creating Shareholder Value* (rev. ed. The Free Press 1998). At some point in your busy schedule, you should make time to read this book, after which you will be well prepared to discuss (and defend) your "flexible commitment" to increasing your emerging company's market cap.

EXECUTIVE COMPENSATION

One of the first questions an experienced microcap investor will ask about your company is,

> *How closely are your top management's goals aligned with my investment goals?*

This query might prompt the response,

> *What are your investment goals?*

To which the experienced microcap investor might reply,

> *I want a return in excess of the S&P 500 that will compensate me for the higher level of risks and transaction costs I assume when I invest in companies like yours. I need to be assured that your pay and incentives appropriately compensate your managers for the risks they take working for an emerging company. Your compensation plan must be structured to hire and retain the kind of people that will grow your market capitalization at a rate appropriate to the risks and costs I am assuming as a shareholder.*

Executive compensation should be tied to financial performance in general, and to share value in particular; however, this policy is not as easily implemented as inexperienced investors think. Shareholders want your board of directors to devote a significant amount of time to establishing executive compensation policies that link short-term performance with a sustained long-term increase in shareholder value. Total compensation generally consists of

1. Base salary.
2. Short-term incentive, such as an annual bonus.
3. Purchase options on listed stock.
4. Shares of restricted stock.

Over the lifetime of any employee, benefits such as health insurance and a pension are important compensation features. When evaluating an emerging company, however, the experienced microcap investor focuses on those elements that provide wealth enhancement for your executives and managers.

Base Salaries

The amount of base salary should reflect experience and sustained performance. A microcap shareholder expects the salaries of your top executives to be set on the basis of the "going market rate" for similar positions within your company's industry sector. As mentioned previously, personnel turnover is a concern of the experienced investor. The turnover rate of key executives is of critical concern. Annual raises for top management must be based more on retention goals than on short-term performances.

The issue of salaries for your top executives can be a source of contention between them and two of your most important groups of stakeholders: your employees and your shareholders. A high degree of discontent within those two constituencies will complicate your march to greater value. This is why experienced investors want the salary portion of any executive's total compensation to provide, over time, the least amount of total compensation.

Annual Bonuses

Conventional wisdom holds that the danger of awarding performance bonuses on an annual basis is that your executives and key managers will focus on short-term goals, at the expense of longer-term objectives. This is a legitimate concern of established companies with "seasoned" stocks. The long-term objective of an emerging company is less complicated than that of a larger-cap corporation. Your long-term goal is to be around. In order to do so, you need to keep your team on board and focused on sustained performance. Here again, bonus plans are as necessary for retention as they are for motivation.

Experienced investors in emerging companies will focus on short-term performance measures. What distinguishes *successful* microcap investors is the short-term performance measures on which they focus. They will understand your industry sector and the short-term performance measures most likely to build long-term value in that particular area of business activity. You have to tie your bonus program to what successful microcap portfolio managers are monitoring. If you are unsure what those measures are for your company, ask some of the portfolio managers.

In Chapter 5 we discuss some of the more common measures that microcap portfolio managers watch: growth in revenues, operating margins, free cash flow, and balance sheet ratios. We discuss the overriding bias among many managers about a quarterly decrease in earnings. You should structure some of your bonus criteria around those investor concerns. We recommend tying most of a bonus to functional performance — that is, to how well a specific department contributes to value enhancement. If your company is a manufacturing company, how well your purchasing department manages the costs and timely delivery of materials may be their key performance objective. Toward the end of Chapter 7 we mention the new products research done by Robert Eccles and PricewaterhouseCoopers: the direct link between new products revenues and market-cap growth. The successful introduction of new products and services is an obvious performance measure for awarding bonuses. All emerging companies operate at a severe risk because they have a narrow customer base; therefore, the acquisition of new customers is an achievement that merits a bonus.

Alfred Rappaport reminds us that, "To be effective, performance measures need to be economically sound, easily understood, and easily tracked." Also, experienced investors do agree that if you institute a bonus program, do not "cap" the payouts. Rappaport is unambiguous: "Such a policy [capping] sends the wrong message to operating units that are otherwise motivated to maximize shareholder value."

Stock Options

Investors have the same concern about granting purchase stock options that they have about bonus payouts: Executives and managers will focus on short-term performance at the expense of building long-term value. We said that experienced microcap investors understood the necessity for some short-term focus when constructing bonus plans. They do not have the same tolerance when it comes to stock options. They want all the stakeholders in your company to prosper, over the long haul. They are very skeptical about the effectiveness of the conventional stock option plans that were common to most emerging companies from the 1990s through 2000. The preponderance of those plans did not ensure survival, much less incremental enhancement of shareholder value. Among those companies that did survive with some increase in market cap, many had stock option plans that were designed to make executives rich for mediocre performance.

Making stock purchase options a substantial part of an executive compensation plan is critical, if you want to demonstrate a commitment to sustaining increases in shareholder value. Emerging company directors often forget that an effective and acceptable stock option plan must be designed in the context of *your investors' opportunity costs.* Most of the prevailing plans over the last decade have not done that.

THE CASE FOR THE HIGHER EXERCISE (STRIKE) PRICE. Microcap investors want a return commensurate with the risks and transaction costs they assumed when they purchased your company's stock. This means the return has to exceed any return that could have been earned by investing in a portfolio indexed to a broad market measure. It also means that the return should exceed any returns that the investor would have received, over like holding periods, from owning the stock of one of your competitors.

A stock option plan, granting a strike price of $20, exercised at the end of four years to acquire shares trading at $25 gives an executive an immediate 25 percent return. Shareholders who bought the stock four years ago at $20 have earned a compounded, annual return of about 5 percent (it is unlikely the microcap company paid dividends.) A plan such as this one obviously doesn't cut it if they could have earned an annual return of 15 percent holding a competitor's stock over the same period.

Your stock option plans must be linked to some alternative investment measure. The original strike price must be adjusted higher than the return of whatever alternative investment measure you select. The measure selected is a matter between you and your shareholders, and perhaps a qualified compensation consultant. It could be a sector or a market index.

Early in Chapter 5 we cite some research about transaction costs. Microcap investors encounter transactions costs that can be 2.5 percent higher than the costs of investing in large-cap stocks. A generally accepted risk premium for microcap stocks is about 5 percent. We recommend that your stock option exercise price be adjusted to reflect an annual return rate at least 8 percent higher than that of the selected market measure.

There always will be someone to challenge both the investment measure and the return premium; however, no one will challenge the strategic initiative for introducing these elements into your stock option plans.

BEHAVIORAL CONSIDERATIONS. There is the probability that the price of your stock won't increase to a level that exceeds the option plan strike price. Or your stock price recedes below the strike price shortly before an exercise date. There have been instances when directors of companies with "underwater" options have lowered (reset) the strike price. We think that this is an acceptable practice, providing that you also compensate your shareholders for any losses they have incurred from holding shares in your company.

There is an issue with respect to option plans now being discussed at some of the prestigious business schools. Some scholars argue that, at some point, even good stock option plans provide diminishing incentives. In this argument, the proponents assume that executives taking advantage of successful plans have too much of their investments in their employer's stock, that is, these executives hold "less than fully diversified investment portfolios." This situation, therefore, creates a cost for a company with a successful plan. That "cost" is the difference between the market value of the shares granted in these plans and the diminishing value placed on those shares by the managers who get them. Our scholars argue that managers began to value their option shares less, as they become more aware of the firm-specific (unsystematic) risk they entail by being overweighted with their company's stock. They have a point. So do the people who advise, "Don't put all your eggs in one basket."

Restricted Securities and Executive Compensation

The experienced investor in any size company prefers a capital structure consisting of just listed stocks and tradable bonds. They understand, however, that emerging companies are likely to require additional financing under special circumstances and provisions. Those circumstances and provisions generally restrict the ownership and the trading of such "special issues." The savvy investor is willing to accept *some* special approaches to *interim* financing as a means to building value, but they won't accept these approaches as "bells and whistles" accoutrements to compensation plans. Don't use any restricted securities in your executive compensation plan.

The SEC provides for using certain stock plans to compensate employees with the amended registration Form S-8, and under the stipulations of amended Rule 401(g) and amended Rule 701. The provisions were intended for OTCBB corporations and for nonreporting companies. They have no relevance for this book's intended audience.

Those special securities for interim financing that investors will accept must *derive* their trading value from the listed securities that make up the capital structure of the corporation. Those tradable securities are often referred to as the "underlying" securities.

SPECIAL AND DERIVATIVE FINANCING

Short-term bank financing may not provide enough money to finance longer-term projects, and an emerging company may need to raise money with special securities. Experienced investors in emerging companies have developed a tolerance for this; however, there are just a few instruments that they will accept. Their acceptance is based on the extent that the instruments enhance the capital structure of the corporation, as well as on the expected return from holding these special securities. They want to be assured that you know what you are doing. You need to understand how to choose what you will use.

Forget about 144A Securities

144A shares of stock are so named after the SEC rule so designated. Rule 144A permits a company under certain circumstances to issue privately placed securities. The SEC restricts the trading of these shares to qualified institutional investors. The illiquid nature of these securities precludes basing their value on the market value of the issuer's common stock. The SEC's policy with respect to 144A stocks is that the decision to hold them is a "question of fact" for the officers of the institutional investors. In other words, it is the investors' call. Institutional investors in emerging companies confront a liquidity challenge when they hold listed shares of microcap stocks. Why do they want to compound the liquidity problem by holding shares whose ownership is limited by SEC dictates? The managers of microcap mutual funds won't touch 144A shares.

Warrants

A stock *warrant* is similar in its provisions to a call option on a stock. A warrant gives its owner the right to purchase shares of a company's stock directly from the company at a fixed price for a given period of time. *A warrant is sold by the company.* The proceeds of the sale go to the company. That is the significant difference between warrants and options. Company stock options are given at no charge in lieu of payments or compensation. Those arrangements can reduce the company's cash outlay, but the company receives no income from such stock option plans. Likewise, companies do not issue "listed" stock options, so a company won't receive any money from the trading of listed options on its stock. Another way warrants differ from options is that warrants have longer times from issue to expiration.

Warrants are used in two ways in corporate finance. Warrants are commonly attached to an issue of a security to enhance the appeal of that security. Your company's IPO or some secondary offerings may have had warrants appended to them. The other use of warrants in raising capital is to issue or sell them separately. There are two main concerns associated with selling warrants separately. One concern is how to price them. The second concern is the impact these warrants will have on the issuing company's capital structure.

There is obviously no reason to undergo the aggravation of issuing stand-alone warrants, unless the money raised is sufficient to meet funding needs for a considerable length of time. The price of each warrant and the quantity of warrants to be issued are the two factors that determine the amount of money raised. The price of the warrant is the overriding factor. That price will be governed by the price of the underlying stock and not necessarily the price at which the stock is trading shortly before the warrants are issued. Reviewing the price range within which the stock has been trading over the past year is an appropriate start to computing the warrant price.

The scope of this book doesn't allow for a description or discussion of derivative pricing. There are scores of articles and books about this matter. In addition to heeding the dictates of financial mathematics, companies should structure warrant issues with a concern for existing shareholders. They are the first people who should be offered the chance to buy the warrants. They have stayed on board when operating capital is tight. They deserve the right of first refusal to the opportunity of leveraging their existing investment. The terms of the issue should balance shareholder appeal with a *reasonable and disciplined* appraisal of exercise/ redemption consequences.

Giving your loyal shareholders a "sweetener" won't mitigate their concern about your financial viability. You need to demonstrate that you are restructuring your operations to ensure redemption at exercise time, without diminishing your critical resources.

When the money from the warrants sale comes in, don't pause for a sigh of relief. You haven't earned the right to do so.

Investors with little emerging company experience (and little overall investment experience) will babble about "earnings dilution" at exercise time. They mean the decrease in earnings per share as a result of stock issued as redemptions. They don't get it, yet. You and your experienced shareholders understand the benefits of more stock in the float.

The redemption effect on shares in the float is also experienced when *convertible* securities get exchanged for authorized shares. The most commonly used instrument in this category is the convertible bond.

Convertible Bonds

A convertible bond can be exchanged for a fixed number of common stock shares, or at a stipulated *conversion price,* during and up to the date the bond matures. There was a period in the 1990s when some renegade financiers structured hybrid convertible debt in a manner that enabled them to profit from the falling prices of an emerging company's shares, and under certain circumstances take control of the company. These situations came to be known as "death spirals." These "toxic converts" are seldom encountered because knowledge of their imbedded perils spread among reputable advisors to emerging companies.

Investment bankers give two reasons why using convertible issues is "good strategy":

1. The company is getting debt on the cheap. The coupon rates can be set below the market rates for straight bonds.

2. At some point in the future, the company can issue stock at a share price higher than the price at which the stock is currently trading.

A FREE LUNCH. The above reasons are supported with arguments like this: "We will underwrite convertible bonds ($1,000 standard face value) at X percent. X percent is currently 150 basis points below what you would have to pay for a straight bond. The conversion provision will be set at 50 shares. Your stock currently trades at $15, so investors buy this convertible with an imbedded value of $750 (50 times $15).

"If your stock price falls and trades below $15 during the period before maturity, they won't convert. As a result you have added to your capital structure at terms well below the market rate. If the stock starts trading much higher than $15, the bond owners will convert. You will issue 50 shares of stock to redeem a bond with a face value of $1,000. You have effectively issued stock at $20, or for one-third more than the current price of $15. Who said there is no such thing as a free lunch?"

OH YEAH? Some experienced shareholders might have a problem with this free lunch. They reason: "So you are saying that after this bond is issued, it can be a good thing that the stock price falls? Get out of here! If you think it's likely that the stock will fall in the near future, let's issue some more common and make hay while the sun shines. AND if the stock goes way up, there are some new shareholders from the conversion who will make out better than us who have been on board for the long haul. Suppose the stock is at $40 when the bonds are converted. Issue plain vanilla bonds so that stock gains wouldn't have to be shared!"

The shareholders' above concerns and objections are legitimate and fitting. The banker's rationale is not all fee-enhancing hype. There is a structure to most convertible debt strategies that can raise needed capital, and assuage existing shareholders. Find it.

The "Message"

The need to reinforce your capital structure with additional long-term financing has sent a message that cannot be diluted: "Our core business activities did not generate enough retained earnings to grow our business." Experienced microcap investors confront this dilemma among almost all of their companies. What determines whether they will remain shareholders *is the manner in which you raise more capital*. They want evidence that you have restructured the company to accommodate the additional costs of this capital. They want assurance that you have a viable plan for reducing the debt components of the new financial structure.

Most importantly they want you to use instruments tied to your existing capital structure: securities that will provide a chance to leverage the return on their initial investment in your company. From your and their shared dilemma, they might still enjoy an increase in value. They want you to make lemonade.

MERGERS AND ACQUISITIONS

Experienced investors, investment bankers, attorneys, consultants, and experienced business leaders are hardly ever in unanimous accord about any aspect of corporate strategy. But they all agree that mergers and acquisitions (M & A) are the most demanding, exacting, and perilous of all corporate activities. Your shareholders will scrutinize your every word, action, response, and reflex once you become engaged in M & A. The road to increased and enhanced shareholder value is strewn with the bones of CEOs who thought they were engineering "A Great Strategic Fit."

Think about the fees your company will pay out to investment bankers, accountants, tax experts, and attorneys.

Think about the compliance and disclosure headaches. Every agency could get involved at some point. There are antitrust issues. There are pooling-of-interest-accounting issues. There can be pollution credit issues. Everybody wants to get in on the act. The Department of Labor (DOL) can sharpen more than one axe on your grinding wheel. They can express concern about arbitrating conflicting union agreements among the merging companies; and your pension fund shareholders may have to defend their votes to DOL's Pension and Welfare Benefits Administration.

You cannot eliminate the subjective. What do the current market values of either company's stock really represent? Over what time lines should incremental cash flows be projected? Is one party's discount rate more appropriate than another party's? What criteria are appropriate for retaining or discharging human resources? What about enhancing a competitive position: Will that position prevail tomorrow in the face of unforeseen change? Regardless of what role religion plays in the lives of you and your directors, M & A considerations are best done while contemplating a higher authority. We are not being sacrilegious. You are bellying up to a buzz saw.

We know of one circumstance in which all shareholders might be in accord with a merger or acquisition. There have been occasions when shareholders unanimously supported a deal that assured the removal of their existing management and directors.

SUMMARY

The three areas of business strategy discussed in this chapter can make or break your company.

1. The professional managers of any investment portfolios expect you and your directors to manage these functions in a reasoned and disciplined manner. A key means to demonstrating commitment to building shareholder value is to align your compensation policies with the interests of your shareholders.

2. Microcap portfolio managers can be tolerant about interim financial difficulties; however, they will not accept a "scramble around" approach to obtaining more funding. They want your efforts to be based on a sound understanding of capital markets and on your obligation not to dilute their opportunities for future returns on their investment.

3. Mergers and acquisitions are complicated. Valuations of the proposed joint enterprises are often speculative. The interests of all the affected stakeholders can be incompatible, even among shareholders of the same company. There is no other instance that will provide you and your directors with the opportunity to demonstrate your worth than in the trying circumstances associated with M & A.

There is no PR spin, nor IR campaign, that will communicate your commitment to increasing shareholder value if you don't demonstrate a reasoned and disciplined approach to directing and managing those three activities. Your actions are what will be measured in decibels.

ALL EMERGING COMPANIES SHARE a common goal: rapid, but sustainable, growth in shareholder equity. The challenge of sustaining this growth is marked with perplexing questions: How can we stay nimble? Do we stick with our core business? How much more do we invest in R & D? Author and consultant James Champy advises that you begin addressing growth issues by identifying the qualities that set you apart. Remind yourself what it was that appealed to your early customers and investors. Always keep those appealing attributes in mind as you plan for growth. Champy warns emerging companies to not do anything that would diminish their unique qualities. He has provided you with an enduring reminder.

We have attempted to provide you with enduring knowledge about how to communicate with investors in a manner that is honest and ethical, as well as legal. The theme of this book was that you must look at the investment world realistically, objectively, and courageously. In rereading our work before sending it to the publisher, we discovered that we had focused on the reality and the objectivity at the expense of courage. Permit us to correct this.

Integrity isn't just financial honesty or conscientious compliance with the law. It is also admitting mistakes and taking responsibility. Doing so publicly is the courageous part of the investor relations process. You surely will have the opportunity to demonstrate that courage to investors, and it will occur sooner rather than later.

No matter what precautions and controls you have to forestall situations that impede your march to growth, your company is going to get whacked by events beyond your control. Experienced investors understand this. They own stock in companies that have experienced recalls, sabotages, strikes, environmental suits, embezzlements, natural disasters, and the threat of technological obsolescence.

Experienced investors expect the unexpected. They want the companies they own to face the unexpected casualty and deal with it, and with all the challenges to growth. They expect their companies to be able to communicate their actions and responses to any challenge as circumstances dictate. When your actions and responses are communicated in a way that demonstrates responsibility, prudence, and good judgment, your experienced investors will stay the course.

More likely, they will be buying when the trepid are selling.

Keep strong, stay brave, have fun!

index